PRESIDENT'S MALARIA INITIATIVE

Uganda

Malaria Operational Plan FY 2016

TABLE OF CONTENTS

ABBREVIATIONS and ACRONYMS

ACT	Artemisinin-based combination therapy
AL	Artemether-lumefantrine
ANC	Antenatal care
AS/AQ	Artesunate/Amodiaquine
BCC	Behavior change communication
CDC	Centers for Disease Control and Prevention
CHAI	Clinton Health Access Initiative
CI	Collaborative improvement
CPHL	Central Public Health Laboratory
DFID	U.K. Department for International Development
DHIS2	District Health Information System 2
DHMT	District Health Management Teams
DHS	Demographic and Health Survey
DOT	Directly observed treatment
DP	Dihydroartemisinin–piperaquine
EPI	Expanded Program on Immunization
EUV	End-use verification
FANC	Focused antenatal care
FETP	Field Epidemiology Training Program
FY	Fiscal year
Global Fund	Global Fund to Fight AIDS, Tuberculosis and Malaria
GoU	Government of Uganda
HC	Health center
Hgb	Hemoglobin
HMIS	Health Management Information System
iCCM	Integrated community case management
IE	Impact Evaluation
IMM	Integrated management of malaria
IPTp	Intermittent preventive treatment in pregnant women
IRS	Indoor residual spraying
ISS	Integrated support supervision
ITN	Insecticide-treated mosquito net
IVM	Integrated vector management
JMS	Joint Medical Stores
M&E	Monitoring and evaluation
MCH	Maternal and child health
MIP	Malaria in pregnancy
MIS	Malaria indicator survey
MoH	Ministry of Health
MOP	Malaria Operational Plan

NDA	National Drug Authority
NGO	Non-governmental organization
NHS	National Health System
NMCP	National Malaria Control Program
NMS	National Medical Stores
OR	Operational research
PCR	Polymerase chain reaction
PCW	Positive control wells
PEPFAR	President's Emergency Plan for HIV/AIDS Relief
PFP	Private for-profit health facilities
PHFP	Public Health Fellowship Program
PMI	President's Malaria Initiative
PMTCT	Prevention of mother-to-child transmission
PNFP	Private not-for-profit health facilities
QA/QC	Quality assurance/quality control
RBM	Roll Back Malaria
RDT	Rapid diagnostic test
RHD	Reproductive Health Division
SP	Sulfadoxine-pyrimethamine
TWG	Thematic Working Group
UCC	Universal coverage campaign
UMRC	Uganda Malaria Research Center
UMRSP	Uganda Malaria Reduction Strategic Plan 2014–2020
UNICEF	United Nations Children's Fund
USAID	United States Agency for International Development
USG	United States Government
VHT	Village Health Team
WHO	World Health Organization

I. EXECUTIVE SUMMARY

When it was launched in 2005, the goal of the President's Malaria Initiative (PMI) was to reduce malaria-related mortality by 50% across 15 high-burden countries in sub-Saharan Africa through a rapid scale-up of four proven and highly effective malaria prevention and treatment measures: insecticide-treated mosquito nets (ITNs); indoor residual spraying (IRS); accurate diagnosis and prompt treatment with artemisinin-based combination therapies (ACTs); and intermittent preventive treatment of pregnant women (IPTp). With the passage of the Tom Lantos and Henry J. Hyde Global Leadership against HIV/AIDS, Tuberculosis, and Malaria Act in 2008, PMI developed a U.S. Government Malaria Strategy for 2009–2014. This strategy included a long-term vision for malaria control in which sustained high coverage with malaria prevention and treatment interventions would progressively lead to malaria-free zones in Africa, with the ultimate goal of worldwide malaria eradication by 2040–2050. Consistent with this strategy and the increase in annual appropriations supporting PMI, four new sub-Saharan African countries and one regional program in the Greater Mekong Subregion of Southeast Asia were added in 2011. The contributions of PMI, together with those of other partners, have led to dramatic improvements in the coverage of malaria control interventions in PMI-supported countries, and all 15 original countries have documented substantial declines in all-cause mortality rates among children less than five years of age.

In 2015, PMI launched the next six-year strategy, setting forth a bold and ambitious goal and objectives. The PMI Strategy 2015–2020 takes into account the progress over the past decade and the new challenges that have arisen. Malaria prevention and control remains a major U.S. foreign assistance objective and PMI's Strategy fully aligns with the U.S. Government's vision of ending preventable child and maternal deaths and ending extreme poverty. It is also in line with the goals articulated in the RBM Partnership's second generation global malaria action plan, *Action and Investment to defeat Malaria (AIM) 2016-2030: for a Malaria-Free World* and WHO's updated *Global Technical Strategy: 2016-2030*. Under the PMI Strategy 2015–2020, the U.S. Government's goal is to work with PMI-supported countries and partners to further reduce malaria deaths and substantially decrease malaria morbidity, towards the long-term goal of elimination.

Uganda was selected as a PMI focus country in FY 2006. This FY 2016 Malaria Operational Plan presents a detailed implementation plan for Uganda, based on the strategies of PMI and the National Malaria Control Program (NMCP). It was developed in consultation with the NMCP and with the participation of national and international partners involved in malaria prevention and control in the country. The activities that PMI is proposing to support fit in well with the NMCP strategic plan and build on investments made by PMI and other partners to improve and expand malaria-related services, including the Global Fund to Fight AIDS, Tuberculosis, and Malaria (Global Fund) malaria grants. This document briefly reviews the current status of malaria control policies and interventions in Uganda, describes progress to date, identifies challenges and unmet needs to achieving the targets of the NMCP and PMI, and provides a description of activities that are planned with FY 2016 funding.

The proposed FY 2016 PMI budget for Uganda is $33 million. PMI will support the following intervention areas with these funds:

Insecticide-treated nets (ITNs): The Uganda Malaria Reduction Strategic Plan 2014–2020 (UMRSP) supports universal access to ITNs through mass campaigns and routine distribution channels, including antenatal care (ANC) clinics, Expanded Program on Immunization (EPI) visits, outreach distribution points, private providers, and commercial outlets.

With FY 2015 funds, PMI will procure 1,096,429 ITNs and distribute 908,776 ITNs (83%) through ANC/EPI clinics, and 187,653 ITNs (17%) through 63 primary schools as outreach distribution points for vulnerable populations. With FY 2016 funds, PMI will procure nearly 2 million ITNs: 800,000 will be distributed through ANC/EPI, 600,000 will be distributed at outreach distribution points and PMI will contribute approximately 600,000 ITNs for the next universal coverage campaign (UCC) expected to take place in 2016/2017. PMI will use mass media and community mobilization strategies to increase knowledge and promote proper and consistent use of ITNs. The combined support from PMI, the Global Fund, and the U.K. Department for International Development (DFID) for the procurement and distribution of ITNs is expected to maintain the high national ITN coverage and use that was achieved through the UCC of 2013/2014.

Indoor residual spraying (IRS): The UMRSP supports scale-up and sustainment of IRS in 45% (50/112) of Ugandan districts. From 2009–2014, PMI implemented IRS in ten high burden districts in the North. As a result, the malaria burden in these districts decreased significantly and PMI shifted its spray operations to target higher burden districts in the eastern region. PMI is supporting spraying in nine eastern districts with high malaria prevalence (Tororo, Lira, Butaleja, Namutumba, Kibuku, Budaka, Pallisa, Bugiri, and Serere) during the 2015 calendar year targeting over 850,000 houses to protect approximately 3 million people. PMI also leveraged funds from DFID to spray an additional five high burden districts in the eastern region in 2015. With FY 2016 funds, PMI will continue to implement IRS in nine eastern districts and plans to use an organophosphate insecticide to ensure prolonged residual and insecticidal effectiveness. PMI will continue to monitor vector behavior and insecticide resistance. Additional focus on behavior change communication (BCC) and malaria surveillance will be given in the former ten districts in the North and the nine new districts in the eastern region to monitor any changes in parasitemia as transition between regions occurs.

Malaria in pregnancy (MIP): With PMI technical support, coordination of MIP-related efforts has improved between the Ministry of Health's Reproductive Health Division and the NMCP, through the establishment of a functional national MIP working group. In 2014, Uganda successfully updated its national MIP policy, guidelines, job aids, and BCC materials to reflect the revised WHO guidance on IPTp. A study looking at the barriers to IPTp uptake was concluded in 2014; the results are helping to inform PMI-supported MIP activities. With FY 2016 funds, PMI will continue to support prevention of malaria in pregnant women through provision of ITNs at ANC clinics, IPTp, and early diagnosis and prompt treatment of MIP. PMI will also strengthen the coordination of ANC workers and continue to provide on-site training and supportive supervision related to MIP in the public and private sector. To increase uptake of IPTp, PMI will work through integrated projects that leverage resources available through the President's Emergency Plan for AIDS Relief (PEPFAR) that support scale-up of prevention of mother-to-child HIV transmission (PMTCT). PMI will continue to provide clean water and drinking cups so that health workers can administer sulfadoxine-pyrimethamine (SP) at ANC clinics as directly observed treatment (DOT).

Case management: The UMRSP objective is to achieve and sustain the target of at least 90% of malaria cases in the public and private sectors and community level receiving diagnosis and prompt treatment according to national guidelines by 2017. Since the launch of PMI, a total of 3.9 million rapid diagnostic tests (RDTs) and 6.2 million ACT treatment doses have been procured. In the past year, PMI has worked to improve diagnostic capacity for malaria and effective case management of febrile illness in 49 districts through training of health care workers in malaria diagnosis and treatment. With FY 2016 funds, PMI will continue to support case management in the public and private sectors. The RDT and ACT commodity gap will be covered with existing FY 2014 and FY 2015 funds. PMI will support integrated community case management (iCCM) in four districts through training, supervision, and commodities procurement. PMI, in collaboration with its partners, will promote the correct use of intravenous artesunate as the first-line treatment for severe malaria. Additionally, with FY 2016 funds, PMI will continue to support the use of RDTs, strengthen quality assurance, and enhance supportive supervision within health centers. Complementing additional resources from other USAID health programs and PEPFAR, PMI will continue to support strengthening the national pharmaceutical management system.

Health systems strengthening and capacity building: In 2012, the Uganda Parliament passed the Wage Bill as a result of the efforts of USAID/Uganda's health systems strengthening activities, which are supported in part through PMI. This has increased the recruitment of staff with relevant professional backgrounds, especially at the health center III and IV levels. As a result, the retention rate of critical staff members at these facilities has increased from 53% in 2011 to 70% in 2013. However, these facilities still face low productivity among health workers and poor attendance. Furthermore, it remains a challenge to motivate recruited health workers who are posted in hard-to-reach areas. With FY 2016 funds, PMI, in collaboration with PEPFAR and other USAID health programs, will continue to support regions and districts to improve performance management, planning, staff training (pre-service and in-service), and service quality. PMI will continue to support the capacity of the NMCP to manage and coordinate multi-sectoral malaria reduction efforts at all levels. PMI will also support four Ugandan nationals through the Field Epidemiology Training Program and three Peace Corps volunteers.

Behavior change communication (BCC): Past PMI activities have reached nearly all Ugandans with key malaria messages on the importance of net use, malaria testing, timely treatment, and prevention of malaria during pregnancy. The communication approaches included radio talk shows and radio spots, interpersonal communication, and educational activities in 200 schools. With FY 2016 funds, PMI will continue to support targeted and evidence-based BCC at the national, district, and community levels. PMI's BCC activities will encourage consistent and proper usage of ITNs, the importance of IPTp, timely testing of all fevers, and appropriate malaria treatment for confirmed cases. In addition, PMI will support communication on iCCM in four districts.

Monitoring and evaluation (M&E): Since 2006, PMI has supported the collection of high quality malaria surveillance data from sentinel sites. The data have been assisting PMI and the NMCP in understanding the effect of interventions and informing current and future strategies. In 2014 these sites transitioned into less resource-intensive malaria reference centers, and were scaled-up to provide wider geographic coverage for the purpose of monitoring key malaria control interventions. In December 2014, Uganda started its second Malaria Indicator Survey (MIS) which was supported by PMI and DFID. Results show a remarkable drop in parasitemia since the last MIS in 2009. With FY 2016 funds, PMI will continue to support malaria surveillance to cover a large geographical area, including districts with changing malaria intervention strategies. PMI will continue leveraging the USG integrated regional health platform for health systems strengthening, and focus on improving the quality and NMCP's use of malaria data. PMI will also continue to support national, regional, district, and health facility level activities including training health workers on new health management information system (HMIS) tools and supportive supervision. In addition, PMI will continue to build the capacity of the NMCP's M&E unit.

Operational research (OR): PMI has been integral in supporting studies related to the improvement of case management and vector control activities to help inform malaria prevention and programmatic policies. Ongoing PMI-supported OR studies include: 1) evaluating the effectiveness of the improvement collaborative approach to improve the quality of health facility data, and 2) improving case management of severe malaria. No operational research studies are planned with FY 2016 funding.

II. STRATEGY

1. Introduction

When it was launched in 2005, the goal of the President's Malaria Initiative (PMI) was to reduce malaria-related mortality by 50% across 15 high-burden countries in sub-Saharan Africa through a rapid scale-up of four proven and highly effective malaria prevention and treatment measures: insecticide-treated mosquito nets (ITNs); indoor residual spraying (IRS); accurate diagnosis and prompt treatment with artemisinin-based combination therapies (ACTs); and intermittent preventive treatment of pregnant women (IPTp). With the passage of the Tom Lantos and Henry J. Hyde Global Leadership against HIV/AIDS, Tuberculosis, and Malaria Act in 2008, PMI developed a U.S. Government Malaria Strategy for 2009–2014. This strategy included a long-term vision for malaria control in which sustained high coverage with malaria prevention and treatment interventions would progressively lead to malaria-free zones in Africa, with the ultimate goal of worldwide malaria eradication by 2040–2050. Consistent with this strategy and the increase in annual appropriations supporting PMI, four new sub-Saharan African countries and one regional program in the Greater Mekong Subregion of Southeast Asia were added in 2011. The contributions of PMI, together with those of other partners, have led to dramatic improvements in the coverage of malaria control interventions in PMI-supported countries, and all 15 original countries have documented substantial declines in all-cause mortality rates among children under five years of age.

In 2015, PMI launched the next six-year strategy, setting forth a bold and ambitious goal and objectives. The PMI Strategy 2015–2020 takes into account the progress over the past decade and the new challenges that have arisen. Malaria prevention and control remains a major U.S. foreign assistance objective and PMI's Strategy fully aligns with the U.S. Government's vision of ending preventable child and maternal deaths and ending extreme poverty. It is also in line with the goals articulated in the RBM Partnership's second generation global malaria action plan, *Action and Investment to defeat Malaria (AIM) 2016-2030: for a Malaria-Free World* and WHO's updated *Global Technical Strategy: 2016-2030*. Under the PMI Strategy 2015–2020, the U.S. Government's goal is to work with PMI-supported countries and partners to further reduce malaria deaths and substantially decrease malaria morbidity, toward the long-term goal of elimination.

Uganda was selected as a PMI focus country in FY 2006. This FY 2016 Malaria Operational Plan (MOP) presents a detailed implementation plan for Uganda, based on the strategies of PMI and the Uganda Malaria Reduction Strategic Plan (UMRSP, 2014–2020). It was developed in consultation with the National Malaria Control Program (NMCP), RBM partners, and with the participation of relevant national and international stakeholders involved in malaria prevention and control in the country. The activities that PMI is proposing to support fit in well with the UMRSP 2014–2020 and build on investments made by PMI and other partners, including the United Kingdom's Department for International Development (DFID) and the Global Fund to Fight AIDS, Tuberculosis, and Malaria (Global Fund), to improve and expand malaria-related services. This document briefly reviews the current status of malaria control policies and interventions in Uganda, describes progress to date, identifies challenges and unmet needs to achieving the targets of NMCP and PMI, and provides a description of activities that are planned with FY 2016 funding.

2. Malaria situation in Uganda

Uganda has the third highest number of *P. falciparum* infections in sub-Saharan Africa, and some of the highest reported malaria transmission rates in the world.[1,2] There is stable, perennial malaria transmission in 90–95% of the country. In the rest of the country, particularly in the highland areas, there is low and unstable transmission with potential for epidemics. According to 2014 data from Uganda's Health Management Information System (HMIS), malaria accounts for 33% (monthly range: 29–38%) of outpatient visits and 30% (monthly range: 24–50%) of hospital admissions. It should be noted that of all the reported malaria cases in 2014, only 39% were laboratory-confirmed.

The most common malaria vectors are *Anopheles gambiae* s.l. and *An. funestus. Anopheles gambiae* s.l.is the dominant species in most places, while *An. funestus* is generally found at sites having permanent water bodies with emergent vegetation. Like *An. gambiae*, it is strongly endophagic and is commonly collected indoors, resting on walls during early morning hours making ITNs and IRS viable vector control strategies. Recently, *An. arabiensis* has been found in northern and eastern Uganda, having been identified from *An. gambiae* s.l. samples. *Anopheles arabiensis* tends to bite earlier in the evening, feeds more willingly on domestic animals, and has a greater propensity to feed outdoors than does *An. gambiae*, but remains an effective malaria vector. Limited sampling from Apac District (in the previous northern IRS zone) indicates that *An. arabiensis* may have replaced *An. gambiae* as the predominant malaria mosquito in this district.[3]

Figure 1:Malaria prevalence by region, 2009 and 2014, Uganda

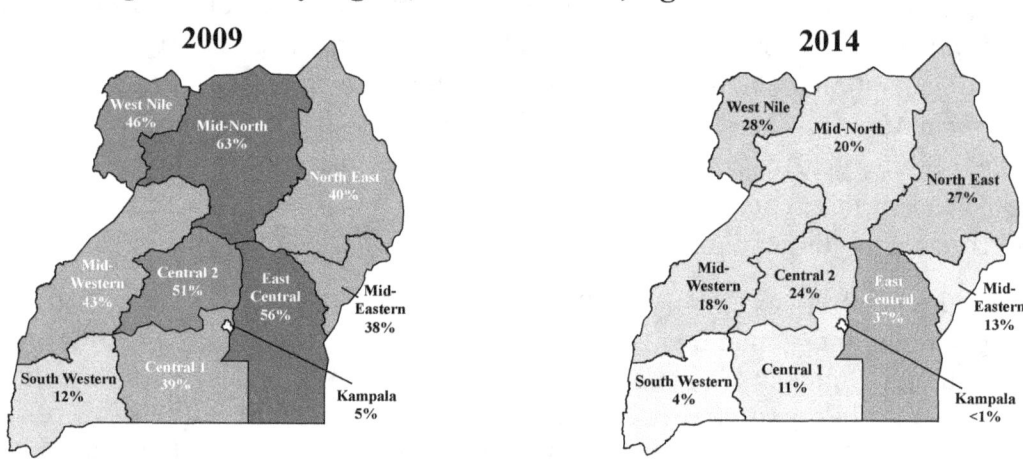

[1]World Health Organization (2014): World Malaria Report. Geneva: WHO.
[2]Okello PE, Van Bortel W, Byaruhanga AM, Correwyn A, Roelants P, et al. (2006) Variation in malaria transmission intensity in seven sites throughout Uganda. Am J Trop Med Hyg 75: 219-225
[3]Okia et al. 2015. Impact of indoor residual spraying (IRS) on malaria vector bionomics in IRS districts compared to a non-IRS district in Northern Uganda. Under review.

Figure 1 shows the percent of children aged 0–59 months that tested positive for malaria by microscopy in the 2009 and 2014 Malaria Indicator Surveys (MIS). Over these five years, the national prevalence went from 42% to 19%. Prevalence was higher in rural areas than in urban areas (22% vs.6% by microscopy) and ranged from 37% in the East Central Region to less than 1% in Kampala. Survey data also indicate that severe anemia (often a result of malaria) is a public health problem in Uganda, though improving; 4.6% of children 0–59 months of age were severely anemic (<8.0 g/dL) in 2014, compared to 9.7% in 2009. In the Mid-North in 2009, severe anemia was the highest in the country at 15.9%, but by 2014, the Mid-North (in which 10 of the 15 districts got carbamate IRS) had dropped to 4.9%.

The Uganda MIS, conducted in late 2014, showed that *Plasmodium falciparum* is the species responsible for the vast majority of malaria cases. *Plasmodium malariae* accounts for less than 1% of cases as a single infection, but is more commonly found as a mixed infection with *P. falciparum* (up to 3% of childhood infections in highly endemic areas). Both *P. vivax* and *P. ovale* are rare and do not exceed 2% of malaria cases in Uganda.

3. Country health system delivery structure and MoH organization

The National Health System (NHS) in Uganda is made up of the public and the private sectors. The public sector includes all government health facilities under the MoH, health services of the Ministries of Defense (Army), Internal Affairs (police and prisons), and Ministry of Local Government. The private health delivery system consists of private health practitioners, private-not-for-profit (PNFP) providers and the traditional and complementary medicine practitioners. The MoH has four levels of administration: the national, regional, district, and county levels. The central level includes the National Directorate of Public Health of the MoH (which houses the NMCP), where national guidelines and norms are promulgated.

The MoH provides leadership for the health sector and is responsible for overseeing the delivery of curative, preventive, palliative, and rehabilitative services to the people of Uganda. The provision of health services in Uganda has been decentralized with districts and health sub-districts playing a key role in the delivery and management of health services at each respective level. The health services are structured into National Referral Hospitals and Regional Referral Hospitals, general hospitals, and health centers (HC) IVs, IIIs, and IIs. The HC I does not have a physical structure but rather consists of a team of people—Village Health Teams (VHTs)—that links health facilities with the community.

These VHT networks facilitate health promotion, service delivery, and community participation in access and utilization of health services. Although VHTs are playing an important role in health care promotion and provision, VHT coverage is still limited. VHTs have been established in 75% of the districts in Uganda but only 31% of the districts have trained VHTs that are operational in all the villages and attrition is high among VHTs. The HC IIs provide the first level of interaction between the formal health sector and the communities. HC IIs only provide outpatient care and community outreach services, and nurses are key to the provision of comprehensive services and linkages with the VHT. The

HC IIIs provide basic preventive and curative care while also providing supportive supervision to the community and HC IIs under their jurisdiction.

4. National malaria control strategy

The Uganda NMCP carried out a midterm review of the 2010–2015 National Malaria Control Strategic Plan and subsequently prepared a six-year UMRSP (2014–2020). The UMRSP has three main goals to be achieved by 2020: 1) reduce annual malaria deaths from 2013 levels to near zero, 2) reduce malaria morbidity to 30 cases per 1,000 population, and 3) reduce malaria parasite prevalence to less than 7%. The UMRSP calls for a rapid and synchronized nationwide scale-up of cost-effective interventions to achieve universal coverage of malaria prevention and treatment. It is a very ambitious strategic plan with a $1.23 billion proposed budget expected to be funded by the Government of Uganda (GoU) with assistance from donors. The UMRSP was developed by a government-led consortium of major donors including PMI and implementing partners.

The objectives of the UMRSP are:

1) By 2017, achieve and sustain protection of at least 85% of the population at risk through recommended malaria prevention measures;
2) By 2018, achieve and sustain at least 90% of malaria cases in the public and private sectors and community level receive prompt treatment according to national guidelines;
3) By 2017, at least 85% of the population practices correct malaria prevention and management measures;
4) By 2016, the program is able to manage and coordinate multi-sectoral malaria reduction efforts at all levels;
5) By 2017, all health facilities and District Health Offices report routinely and timely on malaria program performance; and
6) By 2017, all malaria epidemic-prone districts have the capacity for epidemic preparedness and response.

The role of the NMCP at the central level continues to be to support the implementation of the UMRSP through policy formulation, setting standards and quality assurance, resource mobilization, capacity development and technical support, malaria epidemic identification and response, coordination of malaria research, and monitoring and evaluation (M&E). The UMRSP calls for vector control through IRS, ITNs, and larviciding according to the WHO guidelines, prevention of malaria in pregnancy (MIP) through ITNs and IPTp, effective case management including parasite-based diagnosis and treatment with ACTs, and M&E of all components of the program.

5. Updates in the strategy section

- **UMRSP launched**: In May 2015, during the commemoration of the eighth World Malaria Day, the UMRSP described above was officially launched by Uganda's MoH.

- **MIS 2014 and Impact Evaluation (IE) 2000–2011**: The MIS and IE were completed in 2014/2015 and showed tremendous progress in malaria control efforts. Dissemination of the MIS results is planned for August 2015. During the dissemination, PMI will ensure that stakeholders are cognizant of the gaps remaining in malaria prevention and treatment, and emphasize that the achievements are fragile. In addition, PMI is using the results from the MIS to guide future PMI activities in Uganda.

- **National census:** The Ugandan 2014 census was completed and a preliminary report indicated that the total population of Uganda is 34,856,813 of which 16,935,456 (49%) and 17,921,357 (51%) are male and female respectively. There are 7,353,427 households in Uganda with an average household size of 4.7 people. The census further revealed that the infant mortality rate is 54 per 1,000 live births and the maternal mortality rate is 438 per 100,000 live births. At the time of MOP writing, the preliminary census report did not include information on the age structure of the Ugandan population.

- **NMCP capacity assessment**: With funding from DFID and technical support from PMI, a capacity assessment of the NMCP was completed in early2015. The assessment indicated an urgent need for strengthening the capacity of the NMCP, including structure and functions involving the recruitment of qualified staff. The assessment also proposed that the MoH elevate the profile of the NMCP to a department of malaria and other vector-borne diseases if the vision of malaria elimination by 2030 is to be achieved. In addition, the assessment proposed the decentralization of planning, programming,and support supervision of malaria service delivery to the districts and regional/zonal levels. The proposed budget for this capacity building action plan is $12.4 million. PMI will continue to collaborate with RBM partners in the efforts to strengthen the capacity of the NMCP based on the assessment results.

- **National VHT assessment**: Village health team members are community volunteers who are selected by communities to provide accurate health information, mobilize communities, and provide linkages to health services. Village health teams provide services at the grassroots community level, and usually have some training on prevention and community mobilization. The assessment indicated the need to review the VHT strategy including policy, selection, training, content, role and responsibility definition, and coordination structures at the national and district level. The assessment recommends regular and predictable payments of VHTs as a key to the sustainability of the program and calls for a clear government financing strategy. PMI has carefully analyzed the assessment and will fund non-salary priority actions as appropriate.

- **Universal ITN coverage campaign:** The completion of Uganda's first universal ITN coverage campaign from May 2013 to August 2014 demonstrated the effective partnership between the GoU and its donors, namely the Global Fund, DFID, World Vision, and PMI. Over 22 million ITNs were distributed to all 112 districts in Uganda using VHTs to reach over 90% of the population.

- **Adoption of revised WHO guidelines on IPTp:** The MoH/NMCP adopted the revised WHO IPTp guidelines in Uganda in 2014. PMI will support the NMCP to facilitate adoption of the guidelines by health workers at the national, district, and community levels. Behavior change communication (BCC) activities will be undertaken using print materials, radio, and TV programs to promote adoption of the new guidelines. The revised guidelines have also been included in the revised integrated management of malaria (IMM) training module and communicated to all stakeholders.

6. Integration, collaboration, and coordination

Over the years, malaria control activities in Uganda have been successfully implemented and the NMCP has benefited from increasing support from various partners. PMI works hand-in-hand with the NMCP and coordinates closely with all malaria partners in Uganda to ensure efforts are harmonized and complementary.

- **Global Fund**: The Global Fund currently focuses its resources for Uganda on the procurement of malaria commodities. Uganda plans to have a universal ITN coverage campaign in 2016/2017 as detailed in the concept note submitted to the Global Fund. The approved grant expires on December 31, 2016 and includes a budget for 11 million ITNs for a mass campaign in 2016/2017. The constraints in total allocated funds for the Uganda malaria component could not allow the Global Fund to finance more ITNs. However, the Global Fund technical review panel considered the universal ITN coverage campaign to be technically sound and important for the country to sustain the gains in malaria control. As a result, an additional six million ITNs for the universal campaign have been registered as "unfunded quality demand" which will be prioritized should the Global Fund raise additional resources. The Global Fund's funding will support the procurement and distribution of ACTs and rapid diagnostic tests (RDTs) for treatment and diagnosis of malaria in 2015/2016. In addition, Uganda had three active Global Fund grants that expired in December 2014. The three grants provided ACTs to the public and PNFP sector, support for integrated community case management (iCCM), procurement of microscopes and scale-up of RDTs, routine distribution of ITNs through antenatal care (ANC) and Expanded Program on Immunization (EPI) clinics, BCC activities, support for strengthening the HMIS, drug and insecticide resistance monitoring, health facility surveys, and basic program support to the NMCP.

- **DFID**: DFID made a commitment in 2010 to significantly increase support for health and malaria control in Uganda. DFID funds supported the procurement and distribution of ITNs for the 2013/14 universal coverage campaign and commodity surveillance program through PMI's implementing partners. In 2014, a special arrangement between the U.S. Agency for International Development (USAID) and DFID allowed the use of PMI's funding mechanisms and implementing partners to scale-up its contribution to malaria control in Uganda. Using DFID funding, PMI scaled up implementation of IRS from 9 districts to 14, increased the number of health workers trained in IMM, and provided capacity building to the NMCP and district health management teams (DHMTs).

- **WHO/Uganda**: WHO provides malaria control technical assistance at the national level including support to M&E (data collection and analysis) and emergency preparedness and response.

- **United Nations Children's Fund (UNICEF)/Uganda**: UNICEF supports activities related to iCCM in 19 districts and strongly advocates for scaling up at the national level.

- **Clinton Health Access Initiative (CHAI)**: CHAI is providing technical assistance to the NMCP to develop a strategy for effective case management including diagnosis and appropriate treatment with ACTs in both the public and private sectors in Uganda.

- **Collaboration within the U.S. Government (USG):** PMI works closely with other USG initiatives including the President's Emergency Plan for HIV/AIDS Relief (PEPFAR), maternal and child health (MCH), the Global Health Security Agenda, and Feed the Future to leverage their resources to better achieve malaria control efforts. In addition, the Uganda Mission is focusing on integration in its health portfolio; PMI has contributed resources in these integrated projects that reach populations that PMI's malaria projects may not adequately reach, thus increasing the effectiveness of PMI funds.

7. PMI goal, objectives, strategic areas, and key indicators

Under the PMI Strategy for 2015–2020, the U.S. Government's goal is to work with PMI-supported countries and partners to further reduce malaria deaths and substantially decrease malaria morbidity, towards the long-term goal of elimination. Building upon the progress to date in PMI-supported countries, PMI will work with NMCPs and partners to accomplish the following objectives by 2020:

1. Reduce malaria mortality by one-third from 2015 levels in PMI-supported countries, achieving a greater than 80% reduction from PMI's original 2000 baseline levels.

2. Reduce malaria morbidity in PMI-supported countries by 40% from 2015 levels.

3. Assist at least five PMI-supported countries to meet the World Health Organization's (WHO) criteria for national or sub-national pre-elimination.[4]

These objectives will be accomplished by emphasizing five core areas of strategic focus:
1. Achieving and sustaining scale of proven interventions
2. Adapting to changing epidemiology and incorporating new tools
3. Improving countries' capacity to collect and use information

---

[4]http://whqlibdoc.who.int/publications/2007/9789241596084_eng.pdf

4. Mitigating risk against the current malaria control gains
5. Building capacity and health systems towards full country ownership

To track progress toward achieving and sustaining scale of proven interventions, PMI will continue to track the key indicators recommended by the Roll Back Malaria Monitoring and Evaluation Reference Group (RBM MERG) as listed below:

- Proportion of households with at least one ITN
- Proportion of households with at least one ITN for every two people
- Proportion of children under five years old who slept under an ITN the previous night
- Proportion of pregnant women who slept under an ITN the previous night
- Proportion of households in targeted districts protected by IRS
- Proportion of children under five years old with fever in the last two weeks for whom advice or treatment was sought
- Proportion of children under five with fever in the last two weeks who had a finger or heel stick
- Proportion receiving an ACT among children under five years old with fever in the last two weeks who received any antimalarial drugs
- Proportion of women who received two or more doses of IPTp for malaria during ANC visits during their last pregnancy

8. Progress on coverage/impact indicators to date

Table 1: Evolution of Key Malaria Indicators in Uganda from 2006to 2014

Indicator	2006 DHS	2009 MIS	2011 DHS	2014 MIS
% Households with at least one ITN	16%	47%	60%	90%
% Households with at least one ITN for every two people	N/A	N/A	N/A	N/A
% Children under five who slept under an ITN the previous night	10%	33%	43%	74%
% Pregnant women who slept under an ITN the previous night	10%	44%	47%	75%
% Households in targeted districts protected by IRS	N/A	N/A	N/A	N/A
% Children under five years old with fever in the last two weeks for whom advice or treatment was sought	N/A	70%	N/A	82%
% Children under five with fever in the last two weeks who had a finger or heel stick	N/A	17%	N/A	36%
% Children receiving an ACT among children under five years old with fever in the last two weeks who received any antimalarial drugs	N/A	23%	N/A	87%
% Women who received two or more doses of IPTp during their last pregnancy in the last two years	16%	32%	25%	45%
Prevalence of parasitemia (by microscopy) in children 0–59 months	N/A	42%	N/A	19%
Prevalence of anemia in children 0–59 months (Hgb<10.9g/dl)[8,9]	73%*	62%	50%	N/A
Prevalence of severe anemia in children 0–59 months (Hgb<8 g/dl)	N/A	10%	N/A	5%

*The DHS 2006 anemia measured children between 6–59 months.

9. Other relevant evidence on progress

Impact Evaluation 2000–2011:

The Uganda IE covering the period from 2000 to 2011 showed a substantial decrease in the proportion of children 6–59 months old with severe anemia (16.7% to 4.7%). All-cause under-five mortality

17

declined from 152/1,000 (DHS 2000) to 90/1,000 (DHS 2011). The evaluation concluded that since a substantial increase in malaria intervention coverage occurred during this time, malaria interventions could have contributed to the observed 41% decline in under-five mortality, taking into account other factors that could also have contributed to the observed reduction such as vitamin A supplementation for both mothers and children, increased deliveries in health facilities, and increases in measles vaccinations.

Reference center data:

Malaria reference centers have been strategically placed across the country in different transmission zones and in old (received IRS between 2009 and November 2014) and new (received IRS after November 2014) IRS districts in order to provide accurate data on the effect of different interventions. Data from reference centers in new IRS districts such as Amolatar (Figure 2) will be used to monitor the effects of IRS, and any additional ITN campaigns. Although difficult to discern as a result of seasonality, data obtained from the reference centers and presented in Figure 2 suggest that from January 2014 – March 2015, IRS was highly effective in reducing test positivity rates.

Figure 2: Malaria test positivity in Amolatar District in Northern Uganda, Jan 2014—March 2015

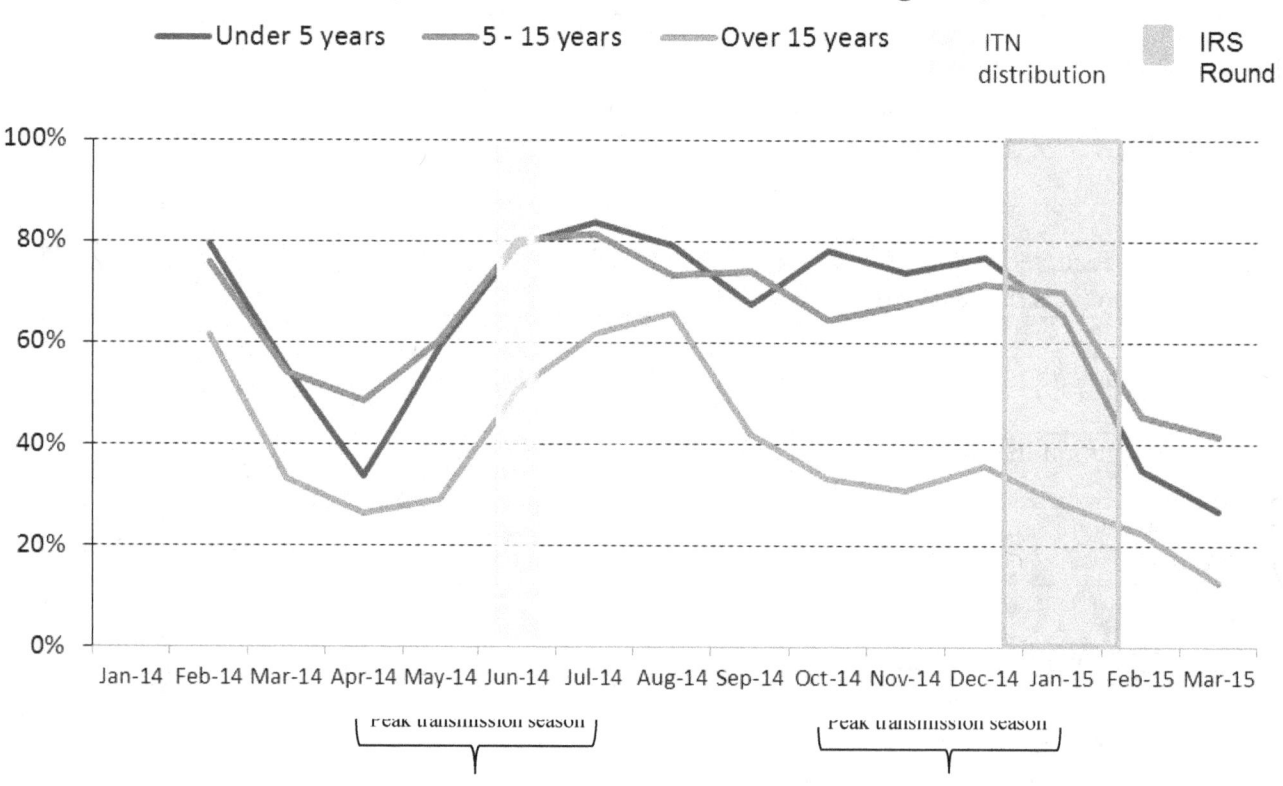

Heath Management Information System (HMIS):

The HMIS provides critical data on malaria-related indicators that are used to assess trends, highlight progress and challenges, and guide PMI's programmatic activities. Since 2013, there has been an improvement in the accuracy, completeness (with about 90% of public facilities reporting), and timeliness of malaria data contributing to the regular preparation of the Uganda malaria quarterly bulletin. The quarterly bulletin includes updates on malaria interventions, malaria burden (national, regional, and district level), and data on laboratory diagnosis, treatment practices, and special topics as needed. As an example, outpatient department data presented in the quarterly bulletin covering January – March 2015 indicated the malaria burden was the lowest it has been since 2013 (Figure 3). The bulletin, which is developed through a collaborative process led by the NMCP, provides an opportunity for the NMCP and malaria stakeholders to monitor and review malaria program performance and to make informed decisions based on this data.

Figure 3: Outpatient department – malaria burden in Uganda

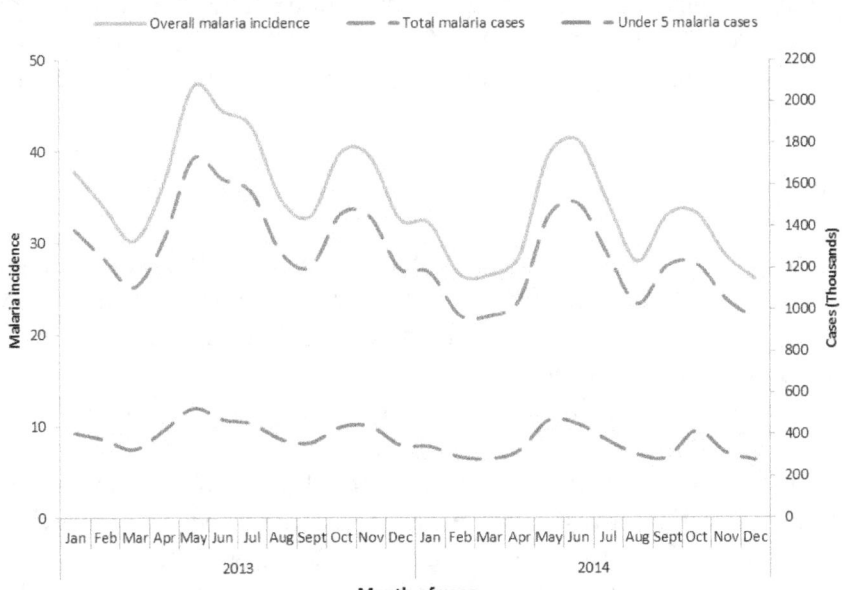

Malaria RDT study:

In collaboration with the Foundation for Innovative New Diagnostics project and with support from Malaria Consortium's Pioneer Project, the Malaria Consortium has evaluated the use, utility, and acceptability of positive control wells (PCWs) for malaria RDTs in two malaria-endemic districts (Kiboga and Kyankwanzi). The study concluded that health workers, including VHTs, correctly perform and interpret PCWs after a half-day training, and maintain this standard over six months of routine use. The PCWs appear to improve health workers' confidence in RDT validity. The PCW may be packaged separately from RDTs and frequency of use is variable. However, there is a need for future operational research (OR) and implementation to provide information on cost-effectiveness.

IPTp2 study:

In light of the low uptake of IPTp2 observed nationally, PMI supported a study to assess the barriers to IPTp2 uptake and to develop recommendations for improvement. The research concluded that, despite a range of minor concerns (for example with regard to taking IPTp on an empty stomach), women and communities have largely positive views of ANC and IPTp. Refusal rates of IPTp are low and given the high ANC attendance figures, the main obstacles to the provision of IPTp are therefore likely to be supply-side challenges. In the past, many health facilities struggled with frequent stockouts of the drug used for IPTp, although this has been improving thanks to recent efforts from the Ministry of Health. Private facilities on the other hand have to buy their own supplies, which means stockouts are still a problem. Another major barrier to the provision of IPTp is health workers' inadequate knowledge with regard to when and how to provide IPTp. This is compounded by the incoherent and out-of-date information provided in many policy documents and job aids that are supposed to guide health workers. Moreover, the policies in use are not in line with the most recent WHO policy recommendations for the provision of IPTp. With PMI support, the policy documents and job aids have since been updated and are in the process of being rolled out.

Malaria program management review:

DFID's 2014 annual program management review showed that over 90% of the population had received nets by the end of the universal coverage campaign (UCC). These results were confirmed by the findings of the 2014 MIS. Review of the malaria control program indicated that IRS implementation started late in 2014 and there were some management challenges at the beginning of the program. By June 2015, 184,638 households had been sprayed with DFID support in five northern Uganda districts. The review highlighted the need for concerted BCC efforts after the UCC, with increased focus on interpersonal communication to ensure utilization and proper care of nets. In addition, the review called for a clear distribution plan that targets the poorest and most vulnerable for additional nets bought with DFID support. The review also mentioned the need for development of clear selection criteria for VHTs to be trained in iCCM, possibly using a weighting system to prioritize those from rural sub-counties. In addition, there is need to institute measures to improve data quality and record-keeping by VHTs through focused supervision. These recommendations were further echoed in the MoH VHT assessment report, and PMI will support their implementation.

10. Challenges and opportunities

Over the past decade, there has been a deliberate effort by the NMCP to improve their approach to malaria control and reduce the disease's impact on the Ugandan population. While much has been achieved, there are notable weaknesses in the implementation of the current malaria strategies which, if unaddressed, would impede progress in reducing the malaria burden in Uganda. These challenges include:

Management challenges

- **Limited capacity of the NMCP**: There are several vacant positions in the NMCP with some filled by junior staff members and others provided by different donors leading to multiple salary schemes that create tensions within the NMCP. In addition, the program has had an acting program manager for the last several years, without full mandate for program implementation affecting implementation of NMCP activities. There is also a lack of regular staff and program reviews, inadequate empowerment of existing staff, and a poor working environment, coupled with the low profile of the NMCP within the MoH structure. The NMCP's capacity is limited by a small budget, and the program has had to significantly rely on support from various malaria stakeholders to implement its activities.
- **Limited engagement of the private sector:** Despite the potential provided by corporate companies to support malaria, there is limited engagement of the private sector.
- **Anti-homosexuality Act:** The 2014 passage and signing of the Anti-Homosexuality Act in Uganda led to a reassessment of the U.S. Government's relationship with the GoU, including the MoH. The reassessment resulted in policy edicts, including guidelines on allowable and non-allowable costs that may be incurred by all USG implementing partners. PMI has taken these measures into account in the FY 2016 MOP, and will continue to ensure that all activities comply with all USG policies.

Program challenges

- **Vector resistance to insecticide:** Vector resistance to insecticides is recognized as an issue in Uganda and may compromise the overall vector control program if not carefully addressed. The NMCP has little capacity for entomologic surveillance, including insecticide susceptibility testing. The NMCP also has limited capacity to oversee and coordinate large-scale IRS operations. Some funding is needed from the MoH to enable the NMCP to contribute to limited insecticide susceptibility testing in four IRS districts of concern in the new southeastern IRS region.
- **Low IPTp uptake:** Although the IPTp policy has been in place for more than ten years, the 2014 MIS indicates that only 59% of pregnant women received one dose of sulfadoxine-pyrimethamine (SP) and only 45% received two or more doses. Given that ANC attendance is high with 94% of women making at least one visit, IPTp rates should be much higher.
- **Poor case management and delayed treatment**: Uganda's case management strategy is to confirm all suspected cases of malaria with RDTs or microscopy and to treat confirmed malaria cases with ACTs while further diagnosing negative malaria cases for other possible causes of fever. However, testing rates are still low, and fever cases that have been confirmed not to be malaria are still treated with antimalarials. Additionally, there have been some instances where there have been significant delays in treating confirmed malaria cases.

- **Poor acceptance of IRS among some communities**: Despite good coverage of IRS, there is still strong community resistance in some areas. However this resistance usually dissipates with appropriate BCC and when people see the effectiveness of IRS.
- **Supply chain challenges in the public sector:** Commodity supply to public sector health facilities remains a major challenge. The Mission has serious issues with the National Medical Stores' (NMS) capacity, accountability, and transparency and will not currently provide malaria and non-malaria USG-procured commodities (PEPFAR, SMGL, RH/FP and other) to the NMS. This chronic problem can be resolved if the capacity, accountability, and transparency of the NMS are improved. For USG-procured commodities to go through the NMS, a major transformation process within the NMS and the MoH is needed. These exercises will need high level advocacy, budgetary, and system support from the GoU. Until the issue is resolved with the NMS, PMI advocates for commodities to reach the public sector through the Joint Medical Stores (JMS) in hard-to-reach areas and in times of outbreaks.

Opportunities
- Implementation of the new UMRSP and M&E plan will provide opportunities to increase the capacity of the NMCP, enabling it to evolve its planning, programming, and supervision roles to the subnational level.
- The results achieved in all malaria indicators (according to the 2014 MIS) have provided motivation for MoH leadership and program managers, donors, implementing partners, health care workers, and all stakeholders to maintain the achieved results and to work toward the pre-elimination phase of malaria in Uganda.
- Potential remains to mobilize private corporations, estate farms/plantations, and health providers to engage in malaria prevention and treatment activities in order to reach a larger proportion of the population.
- The MoH has committed to improve: 1) NMCP's organizational, structural, and functional capacities based on the NMCP capacity assessment carried out in 2015; and 2) VHT's structural and functional capacity to the level of paid community health extension workers from the current purely voluntary services.

III. OPERATIONAL PLAN

PMI supports all elements of the NMCP's national malaria strategy, with the exception of larviciding and environmental management.

1. Insecticide-treated nets

NMCP/PMI objectives

The UMRSP objective for vector control is to achieve and sustain protection of at least 85% of the population at risk through recommended malaria prevention measures (ITNs, IRS, and larval source management) by 2017. The specific objective for nets is to maintain universal access to long-lasting ITNs in all transmission settings and control stages, resulting in a minimum of 85% of households with at least one long-lasting ITN for every two persons. There was a strategic shift a few years ago from targeted mass ITN distribution campaigns (focused on pregnant women and children under five) to UCCs where one ITN is distributed for every two persons. Uganda completed its first UCC in 2014 and plans to repeat a UCC every three years, with the next campaign taking place in 2016/2017. Universal coverage will be maintained through a continuous distribution system as indicated in the policy that employs a range of delivery channels including: 1) free ITN distribution through ANC and EPI clinics, 2) free ITN distribution using schools as outreach distribution points for vulnerable populations in hard-to-reach areas, 3) sale of subsidized ITNs through the private sector (social marketing), and 4) commercial sale of ITNs at full cost. Despite the multiple continuous distribution channels, selected schools, social marketing, and commercial sales have not been operational to date; distribution so far has been limited to mass campaign and ANC/EPI clinics.

Progress since PMI was launched

Since 2006, PMI has procured 11,716,493 and distributed 11,499,857 ITNs, mainly through the UCC campaign of 2013/14 (7,050,000 ITNs) and also to pregnant women and children under five years of age through targeted mass net distribution campaigns, and ANC/EPI clinics, (4,449,857 ITNs). There has also been limited distribution by NGOs and CSOs such as World Vision and The AIDS Support Organization (TASO) through mass campaigns, and through ANC and EPI clinics supported by the Global Fund, by large company corporate social responsibility programs, and by private donations. PMI has also supported BCC efforts to increase demand for and promote correct use of ITNs. This effort, combined with ITNs supported by the Global Fund and DFID, has increased the national household ownership of ITNs to 90% (MIS 2014). PMI has already achieved its target of net ownership in Uganda. Now it is critical to maintain this achievement, and continue to increase net use.

23

Progress during the last 12–18 months

With support from the Global Fund, PMI, and DFID, the UCC was launched in May 2013 and completed in August 2014. The campaign successfully distributed over 22 million ITNs reaching over 7 million households. The GoU provided security coverage to ensure the nets reached their intended distribution sites from the central, district, and sub-county warehouses, and that ITNs were distributed in a safe and secure manner at each point of distribution.

At the request of the NMCP/MoH and donors (Global Fund, DFID, WHO, and World Vision), PMI led the ITN distribution for the UCC. In this role, PMI mobilized 890 district leaders, 5,933 sub-county leaders, and 16,415 community leaders to provide support for the net distribution. PMI also trained 488 district task force members, 804 sub-county supervisors, and 32,830 VHTs to oversee and undertake the distribution activities. The door-to-door approach used during the campaign significantly increased net ownership throughout Uganda.

In addition to providing technical support to the UCC, PMI also procured 1,752,577 ITNs and distributed 114,930 ITNs through ANC/EPI and 1,637,647 through the campaign in FY 2014.

As outlined in the FY 2014/15 MOPs, PMI planned to support selected schools as outreach distribution points for continuous distribution in hard-to-reach areas without a nearby health center, based on the child's household composition. Schools will be used to promote consistent and correct use of ITNs at the household level using parent and teachers' associations (PTAs), teachers and students as change agents. However, this channel has not yet been operationalized.

Results from the 2014 MIS show that Uganda has achieved its PMI net ownership target of 85% of households with at least one ITN. Uganda has also made great progress in ITN use among vulnerable groups, with use among children under five years of age currently at 74% (MIS 2014) compared to 33% in the 2009 MIS.[5] The ITN use among pregnant women is at 75% compared with 44% in 2009. PMI conducted a qualitative assessment on ITN care and repair in 2014 in two districts in central eastern Uganda. The assessment found that prolonging net durability through care and repair has important implications for : 1) reducing both malaria transmission and the frequency of net replacement, 2) protective behavior, which offers promise for improving net integrity and durability, 3) potential cost-savings and public health benefit associated with extending the useful life of ITNs, and 4) prevention and mitigation of damage, which will become ever more critical to ensuring adequate net coverage at the population level. The results revealed that net damage was common and the most cited causes were children and rodents. Responses exposed both aesthetics and malaria protection as important factors when deciding whether, when, and how to care for and repair nets. The study recommended that BCC should continue to emphasize the importance of maintaining net integrity for malaria prevention

---

[5] The President's Malaria Initiative Eighth Annual Report to Congress 2014

purposes as well as for maintaining aesthetic appeal, and PMI's BCC activities will be updated to reflect the findings of the study[6].

In 2015, PMI plans to conduct prospective ITN monitoring to determine the survivorship, attrition, and bio-efficacy of nets that are already planned to be distributed (ITNs going to northern Uganda to assist with the current upsurge or replacement ITNs for districts which received ITNs during the UCC pilot in 2012). The protocol is currently under development, however the study will follow PMI guidelines for net durability monitoring. For further details, see the *Monitoring & Evaluation* section.

Commodity gap analysis

Table 2: ITN Gap Analysis

Calendar Year	2015	2016	2017
Total targeted population[1]	35,800,000	36,831,040	37,891,774
Continuous Distribution Needs			
Channel #1: ANC[2]	1,790,000	1,841,552	1,894,589
Channel #2: EPI[3]	1,432,000	1,473,242	1,515,671
Channel #3: Outreach distribution points for vulnerable populations	187,653	350,000	600,000[4]
Channel #4: Replacement ITNs from 2012 UCC pilot[5]	1,200,000	-	-
Estimated Total Need for Continuous	4,609,653	3,664,794	4,010,260
Mass Distribution Needs			
2016 mass distribution campaign			
Estimated Total Need for Campaigns	-	20,461,689	-
Total Calculated Need: Routine and Campaign	**4,609,653**	**24,126,483**	**4,010,260**
Partner Contributions			
ITNs carried over from previous year	0	0	0
ITNs from MoH	0	0	0
ITNs from Global Fund (New Funding Model)	1,000,000[6]	17,000,000	500,000[8]
ITNs from other donors (DFID)[7]	1,600,000	5,000,000	1,000,000[8]
ITNs planned with PMI funding	1,000,000	1,096,429	1,991,632
Total ITNs Available	**3,600,000**	**23,096,429**	**3,491,632**
Total ITN Surplus (Gap)	**(1,009,653)**	**(1,030,054)**	**(518,628)**

---

[6]   is about how the net looks: a qualitative study of perceptions and practices related to mosquito net care and repair in two districts in eastern Uganda

Footnotes: [1]*Total targeted population is based on the 2014 national census data, adjusted for 2.88% annual population growth.* [2]*Assuming 5% of the population becomes pregnant.* [3]*Assuming 4% of the population are children under five years of age.*[4]*For outreach distributions to vulnerable populations in 200 hard-to-reach schools, assuming approximately 3,000 ITNs/school.*[5]*Four districts had benefited from a PMI pilot UCC ITN distribution campaign in September 2012. The nets are more than three years old and therefore need to be replaced.*[6]*Global Fund nets though The AIDS Support Organization.*[7]*Exact figures are not yet known.*[8]*PMI will distribute 591,632 and 1.4 million ITNs through UCC and ANC/EPI clinics and schools respectively; and the 1.5 million ITNs from the Global Fund and DFID will be distributed through ANC/EPI clinics as well.*

Plans and justification

PMI will continue to support the NMCP in maintaining high ITN ownership and use to stay at the 85% target through routine distribution of ITNs in 2015 and 2016 through ANC, EPI, and through schools as outreach distribution points in hard-to-reach areas. With FY 2016 funds, PMI will distribute 1.4 million ITNs through ANC/EPI clinics and selected schools; and approximately 500,000 and 1,500,000 ITNs from the Global Fund and DFID respectively will be distributed through ANC/EPI clinics as well.

PMI will also procure ITNs to support the next UCC of 2016/17. PMI will contribute 1,096,429 in the early phase of the UCC (October-November 2016) from the FY 2015 MOP. PMI will also contribute 591,632 ITNs from the FY 2016 MOP to the later phase of the UCC 2017 (January-June 2017).Overall, approximately 20.5 million nets are needed for the 2016/17 UCC campaign, of which the Global Fund will be providing 17 million, PMI will provide approximately 1.7 million (FY 2015 and FY 2016 MOPs combined), and the remaining ITNs are expected to be covered through other donors, including DFID.

PMI will continue its efforts to increase net usage through community-based BCC at schools and health facilities, and will support the NMCP to strengthen the Integrated Vector Management (IVM) Thematic Working Group (TWG) to harmonize ITN programs across stakeholders. While the Global Fund will procure the bulk of the ITNs for the next UCC, PMI and DFID will primarily supply ITNs for continuous distribution to maintain high ITN ownership.

Proposed activities with FY 2016 funding: ($9,500,084)

- **Procurement of ITNs:** PMI will procure approximately 1,991,632 ITNs for distribution through the 2016/17 UCC (591,632 ITNs); ANC and EPI clinics (800,000 ITNs) and schools as outreach distribution points for vulnerable populations (600,000 ITNs). Costs include procurement, shipping, transportation, country clearances, and warehousing. ($7,110,126)
- **ITN distribution for the 2016/17 UCC:** This funding will cover the distribution costs of the 591,632 ITNs for the UCC. ($709,958)
- **ITN distribution to hard-to-reach vulnerable populations through schools:** PMI will procure approximately 600,000 ITNs to be distributed to hard-to-reach vulnerable populations (pregnant women and children under five) through schools. Schools present a promising opportunity to distribute nets to a wide range of households on a yearly basis. Lesssons learned from school-based distributions in other countries (Tanzania, Nigeria, and Senegal) on training and logistics are being

taken into consideration. In Uganda, the schools will to be selected in hard-to-reach areas where health facilities with ANC/EPI services are not available within the vicinity. Each target school will distribute approximately 3,000 ITNs per year. The schools will serve as ITN distribution points for continuous distribution and for promotion of consistent and correct use of ITNs. ($720,000).

- **ITN distribution through ANC and EPI clinics:** PMI will support the continuous distribution of ITNs through ANC and EPI clinics to maintain the high net ownership achieved and increase the use of nets by vulnerable groups. These funds support the distribution of 800,000 free ITNs via ANC and EPI clinics. ($960,000)
- **BCC on net utilization**: Based on the findings of the study on net care and repair, PMI will support BCC to emphasize the importance of maintaining net integrity for malaria prevention purposes. With FY 2016 funds, PMI will support community, school, and health facility level BCC activities. (*See BCC section for details on activities and funding*)
- **Monitoring for net attrition, survival, physical integrity, and bioefficacy**: This will be the third and final year of funding for this monitoring project. (*See M&E section for details on activities and funding*)

2. Indoor residual spraying

NMCP/PMI objectives

IRS is a proven intervention and a key component of the UMRSP, which recommends that IRS coupled with routine entomological monitoring and vector susceptibility studies be scaled-up in a phased and contiguous manner in 50 districts with the highest transmission rates. While the NMCP planned to spray two districts in 2014/2015, along with the nine districts supported by PMI and five supported by DFID, sufficient operational funds to implement IRS have not yet been identified. An IVM TWG chaired by the PMI IRS implementing partner supports IRS efforts in Uganda, and works with the NMCP to review and develop national malaria surveillance and control strategies.

Progress since PMI was launched

In Uganda, pilot IRS projects began in urban areas, particularly Kampala, in the 1940s with dramatic reduction of disease transmission.[7] However, IRS was only sporadically used through the 1960s. In 2006, PMI supported a large-scale IRS program in the epidemic-prone southwestern highland district of Kabale and achieved good coverage and impact results. The following year, PMI shifted operations to Kabale's high-risk sub-counties and extended support to the neighboring district of Kanungu and four northern districts (Kitgum, Pader, Gulu, and Amuru districts) to protect large populations of internally displaced persons.

---

[7]WHO Regional Office for Africa. 2007. Implementation of Indoor Residual Spraying of Insecticides for Malaria Control in the WHO African Region Report. Vector Biology and Control Unit Division of Healthy Environments and Sustainable Development.

From 2009 through 2014, PMI supported blanket IRS in ten northern districts: Kitgum, Agago, Lamwo, Pader, Amuru, Nwoya, Gulu, Oyam, Kole, and Apac, achieving consistently high coverage (above 90%). IRS transitioned to carbamate insecticides in mid-2010 due to the emergence of widespread pyrethroid resistance. Resistance to carbamate insecticides was detected in one site and suspected resistance was found in another two sites during the 2013 national susceptibility survey, prompting a change to an organophosphate insecticide for the 2016 spray season.

Data from PMI-supported reference centers and HMIS (2010 – 2014) have shown strong downward trends of malaria cases in PMI's original ten northern IRS districts. As further evidence of the impact of IRS in Uganda, the 2011 anemia and parasitemia survey comparing IRS to non-IRS districts showed significant improvements in both parasitemia (45% reduction) and anemia (32% reduction) in the IRS districts.[8]

PMI has built the capacity of five private organizations including Kakira Sugar Works, Hima Cement, Kijuura Tea Estates, Tullow Oil, and Kinyara Sugar Works, to conduct IRS in their staff quarters and neighboring communities. Training for company workers on the proper techniques pertaining to IRS safety, insecticide application, hand sprayer maintenance, accountability, and record-keeping is planned for September 2015. This will contribute to an increase in the number of households protected through IRS in the country. Additional training has been given to private pest control companies in workshops held by the PMI IRS implementing partner. Over the last three years, a total of 80 private pest control operators have been trained in IRS management, enabling them to offer IRS to a wider range of households.

Progress during the last 12–18 months

In 2014, PMI conducted its final two spray rounds in ten northern districts with a carbamate insecticide covering 844,576 houses and protecting 2,532,297 people at a coverage rate of over 90%. In 2015, PMI will fully transition to nine new IRS districts to the southeast (Lira, Tororo, Butaleja, Namutumba, Kibuku, Budaka, Pallisa, Bugiri, and Serere). Each district will be blanket sprayed twice in 2015 using a carbamate insecticide. The first spray round for the new districts occurred in two phases, and while low coverage was experienced in the first phase (December 2014 – February 2015), coverage improved dramatically in the second phase (final coverage data pending). The initial low coverage was driven by strong resistance in some of the new districts due to interference from local politicians and certain religious sects, insufficient time to complete community mobilization, and resistance from a few organic farmers.

A summary of the PMI-supported IRS campaigns is shown in Table 3. In addition, DFID funding in 2015 will be used to spray five districts (Alebtong, Dokolo, Amolatar, Kaberamaido, and Otuke) on the southeastern border of the previous IRS districts in the north.

---

[8]Steinhardt LC, Adoke Y, Nasr S, Wiegand RE, Rubahika D, Serwanga A, Wanzira H, Lavoy G, Kamya M, Dorsey G, Filler S: The effect of indoor residual spraying on malaria and anaemia in a high transmission area of Northern Uganda. Am Trop Med Hyg 2013, 88:855-861 doi:10.4269/ajtmh.12-0747.

PMI and the NMCP decided to transition to new southeast districts after 2013/2014 HMIS data revealed a reduction of cases in the Mid-North Region of 66% from 2008/2009 levels. In addition, the 2014 MIS showed that parasitemia in the 15 Mid-North districts decreased from 63% in 2009 to 20% in 2014, a reduction of 68%; in the 10 former IRS districts of the Mid-North region, the parasitemia was reduced to 7% (Table 4). The new southeastern IRS districts were shown to have a prevalence of 36%, nearly twice the national average; this will serve as the baseline for the next MIS in 2018 after they have received several rounds of IRS. A universal coverage campaign was completed in 2014 and initial results from the 2014 MIS indicate high ITN coverage (90%) and use (75%) nationally. It is hoped that ITNs, if used consistently and properly, will be able to maintain the reduction in malaria achieved in PMI's former IRS districts, which will be monitored through enhanced entomological and epidemiological surveillance.

Table 3: Uganda IRS Activities, Districts, and Insecticide Class

Year	Number of Districts	Insecticide Used	Number of Structures	Coverage Rate	Population Protected
2006	1	Pyrethroid	103,329	96%	488,500
2007	5	Pyrethroid	446,117	98%	1,866,000
2008	6	DDT, Pyrethroid	416,452	93%	1,545,000
2009	6	Pyrethroid	850,000	95%	3,000,000
2010	10	Pyrethroid, Carbamate	847,469	99%	2,679,000
2011	10	Carbamate	885,716	99%	2,805,000
2012	10	Carbamate	765,661	90%	2,338,000
2013	10	Carbamate	870,943	97%	2,582,000
2014	10	Carbamate	844,576	90%	2,532,000
2015[1]	9	Carbamate	850,000	TBD	3,000,000
2016[2]	9	Organophosphate	850,000	95%+	3,000,000
2017[2]	9	Organophosphate	850,000	95%+	3,000,000

[1] Based on 2015 work plan targets; current campaign is ongoing.
[2] Projected targets based on national strategic plan and/or discussions with NMCP

The PMI-funded insectary in Gulu was used to rear field-collected mosquito larvae for adult identification and as a training space for Gulu University and MoH personnel for mosquito identification, bioassay training for resistance detection in malaria mosquitoes (WHO and Centers for Disease Control and Prevention (CDC) bottle), and for testing field-caught mosquitoes for insecticide susceptibility by the implementing partner and university collaborators. A MENTOR Initiative insectary in Tororo District was supported by PMI to produce susceptible Kisumu strain *An. gambiae* mosquitoes for southeastern IRS operations in 2015, while providing mosquitoes for IRS quality assurance (QA) testing of sprayed surfaces for several northern districts, reducing the logistical burden of support from Gulu. To further facilitate IRS QA testing and insecticide longevity investigations in southeastern Uganda, the IRS implementing partner is developing a new insectary near field headquarters in Tororo.

Insecticide decay monitoring of PMI's IRS campaign was conducted in Gulu District in 2014. All surfaces (brick, mud + wattle, painted plaster), sprayed with bendiocarb killed at least 85% of susceptible test mosquitoes at the end of 4 months. Five months post-spray in Apac District revealed 95% control on mud + wattle and plain brick walls. Bendiocarb-sprayed painted plaster walls maintained 100% residual kill through September (spray was in April, 2014). Bendiocarb was sprayed from mid-December 2014 to mid-February 2015, and monitored for residual efficacy in three IRS districts (Kaberamaido, Lira, Tororo). Three wall surface types were monitored monthly using 30 susceptible *An. gambiae* Kisumu mosquitoes per wall type in each district. Test results from May 2015 demonstrated 100% mortality on all wall surfaces in all districts, showing full efficacy through three months. Quality assurance testing of sprayed surfaces using cone bioassays within the first two weeks of IRS demonstrated 100% kill at all tested sites.

Table 4: Uganda MIS parasitemia results, 2014 and 2009

Region	2014		2009		% decrease (microscopy)
	Positive RDT	Positive Microscopy	Positive RDT	Positive Microscopy	
Previous IRS districts*	15.1	7.2	80.1	62.5	89
Central 1	13.0	10.5	44.6	39.1	73
Central 2	33.1	23.6	62.1	50.7	54
East Central	49.2	36.5	65.2	56.2	35
Kampala	3.7	0.4	7.4	4.9	92
Mid-North	34.2	20.0	80.1	62.5	68
Mid-Western	17.6	17.8	48.4	42.7	58
Mid-Eastern	26.6	13.4	40.1	37.5	64
North East	55.7	27.3	54.5	40.0	32
South Western	5.7	4.1	17.7	11.6	65
West Nile	51.3	27.5	60.2	45.7	40

*Parasitemia results from 2009 for the previous 10 IRS districts in the Mid-North are inferred from the entire 15-district area, while results from 2014 are specifically for those 10 districts.

PMI has supported comprehensive vector resistance monitoring in six different eco-epidemiological zones throughout Uganda biennially. The last survey occurred in September 2013 with the next one occurring in September 2015. Beginning in 2015, surveys will occur every year. Below are the most recent results from a sample of the four WHO-recommended insecticide classes tested in the six sites (Table 5).

Table 5: Sample of 2013 WHO tube bioassays of *Anopheles gambiae* s.l. against four classes of selected insecticides from six districts around Uganda (mortality range)*

Insecticide	Sites surveyed	# sites resistant, mortality <90%	# suspected resistance, mortality 90-97%	# sites susceptible, mortality ≥98%
Deltamethrin[1]	6/6	6/6 (18-82)	0/6	0/6
Permethrin[1]	4/6	4/4 (24-85)	0/4	0/4
Lambdacyhalothrin[1]	4/6	4/4 (21-56)	0/4	0/4
DDT[2]	6/6	5/6 (10-81)	1/6 (95)	0/6
Bendiocarb[3]	6/6	1/6 (85)	2/6 (94,95)	3/6
Pirimiphos-methyl[4]	6/6	0/6	0/6	6/6

*Includes testing of adults reared from field-collected larvae.
Insecticide classes: 1 = pyrethroid, 2 = organochlorine, 3 = carbamate, 4 = organophosphate

Additional preliminary analysis of intensity bioassays conducted by PMI in 2015 show some resistance to high intensity (5x, 10x) insecticide dosing of *An. gambiae* to permethrin (5x: 9.1%) and deltamethrin (5x: 14.3%; 10x: 14.8%) in Tororo District. Synergist bioassays using PBO increased mortality in *An. gambiae* in Lira and Soroti districts from <90% to near 100%, demonstrating the presence of oxidase activity in detoxification of pyrethroid insecticide. Bendiocarb still retained full susceptibility according to these preliminary intensity assay results.

Plans and justification

With FY 2016 funds, PMI will continue to support the NMCP to implement IRS in nine eastern districts in Uganda i.e. Lira, Serere, Pallisa, Kibuku, Budaka, Namutumba, Butaleja, Tororo, and Bugiri, targeting approximately 850,000 structures and three million people to further drive down parasitemia rates. During this period, DFID will continue to provide funding for IRS in five districts (Otuke, Alebtong, Dokolo, Amolatar, and Kaberamaido) contiguous with former and new PMI IRS districts. Geographically, the DFID-funded districts and the new PMI districts connect Lira and Tororo which make up the northwestern and southeastern borders, respectively, of the new IRS geographical area, forming an IRS corridor targeting high burden districts (Figure 4). If insecticide prices decrease and/or resistance tests allow for switching back to a cheaper insecticide in 2017, PMI, working with the NMCP, may expand operations to new high burden districts contiguous with the existing 14 IRS districts.

PMI will promote best practices where the private sector has initiated, funded, and managed successful IRS programs, most frequently led by the mining and agricultural industries and in partnership with the NMCP. PMI will provide technical guidance on IRS equipment maintenance, spray operations, and insecticide selection to industries currently providing IRS on work sites and in surrounding communities. Industrial and agricultural partners being targeted include Kakira Sugar Works, Hima Cement, Kijuura Tea Estates, Tullow Oil, and Kinyara Sugar Works; PMI is actively looking to expand this engagement.

Figure 4. IRS map showing time period and district transition from the Mid-North Region to the Southeast Region for PMI and DFID districts.

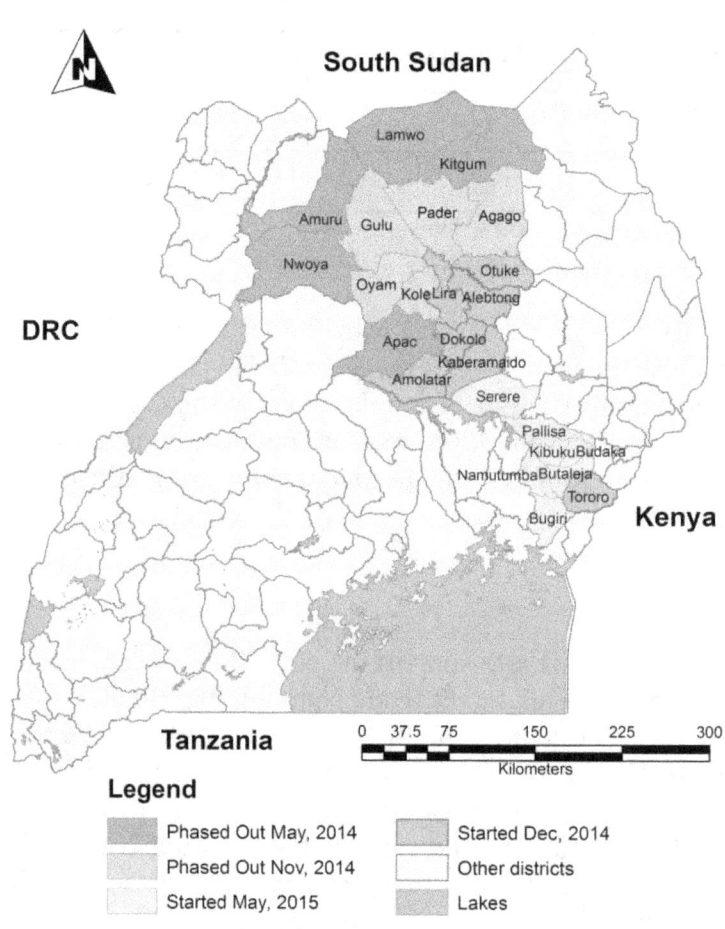

Proposed activities with FY 2016 funding: ($12,392,500)

- **Support IRS**: PMI will continue a second year of IRS in nine eastern districts with a long-lasting OP to which *An. gambiae* s.l is completely susceptible in all areas of Uganda, reducing the yearly spray cycle from two to one. The cost includes all components of IRS: insecticide procurement, spray pumps and other required equipment, logistics, environmental assessments, monitoring, and BCC activities specific to IRS. ($12,243,500)
- **Develop local capacity to expand and sustain IRS**: PMI will continue to use the available private sector opportunities in Uganda to support evidence-based IRS through effective partnership with the private sector in collaboration with the MoH/NMCP. PMI will support the NMCP to promote and increase private sector engagement and investment in IRS through improving their technical expertise and knowledge of IRS best practices to protect employees (settled in their large tea, coffee, and cotton plantations/estates) and the surrounding communities from malaria. Through this initiative, PMI will reach an estimated 10,560 households through six large private companies. PMI will also support capacity building of the DHMTs in the IRS districts to be able to conduct entomological monitoring and other aspects of IRS. ($100,000)
- **Entomology equipment and supplies**: Insecticide resistance monitoring supplies, insectary support (equipment and supplies) for the Gulu, Vector Control Division and Tororo insectaries. Polymerase chain reaction (PCR) reagents as needed by CDC or Makerere University personnel to identify *An. gambiae* complex mosquitoes from field collections and from the annual six sentinel site susceptibility surveys. ($20,000)
- **Two TDYs from CDC/Atlanta**: CDC entomological staff will provide technical support for planning and monitoring IRS activities. Support includes testing for resistance mechanisms in *An. gambiae* and *An. funestus*, training in CDC bottle intensity assays, field collection of mosquitoes for PCR identification of sibling species to monitor population shifts in IRS and former IRS districts, and mosquito surveillance and resistance training for MoH personnel. ($29,000)

3. Malaria in pregnancy

NMCP/PMI objectives

The UMRSP calls for all pregnant women to be treated with effective antimalarial medicine under medical supervision and have access to ITNs. Pregnant women who present with a fever are tested for malaria using microscopy or RDTs, and treated for malaria if the test results are positive or if the cause of fever cannot be determined. Oral quinine is used for treatment of uncomplicated MIP in the first trimester, and ACTs are recommended for use in the second and third trimesters. Parenteral artesunate or quinine is used to treat severe MIP during all trimesters. The objectives of the NMCP for the prevention of MIP are to:

- Ensure every pregnant woman sleeps under an ITN throughout her pregnancy and thereafter.

- Ensure pregnant women receive at least three IPTp doses with an appropriate antimalarial drug and receive early diagnosis and prompt management of malaria episodes.

With PMI's support, Uganda's national policy has already aligned to the new WHO guidance that IPTp should be given at every scheduled ANC visit beginning with the second trimester, if not administered in the prior four weeks.[9] In addition, the policy states that folic acid at a daily dose equal or above 5mg should not be given together with SP as this counteracts its efficacy as an antimalarial. The policy recommends daily iron (30-60mg) and folic acid (0.4mg) supplementation in pregnant women; however these revised dosages have not yet been fully implemented in Uganda. PMI will support the NMCP to 1) disseminate the updated MIP documents and train health workers according to WHO recommendations, 2) advocate for, coordinate, and ensure that 0.4mg folic acid, and 30-60mg iron are procured and distributed, and 3) promote the new iron and folic acid doses for daily use by pregnant women at ANC clinics.

The MoH's Reproductive Health Division (RHD) is currently the lead for operationalizing IPTp by integrating within the Focused Antenatal Care (FANC) policy, which recommends that women with a normal pregnancy make four visits to an ANC clinic prior to delivery and promotes the intake of iron and folic acid supplements among pregnant women according to the newly updated policy and guideline.

The 2014 midterm review reported the need for full integration of the IPTp program within the RHD, leaving the NMCP responsible for providing technical assistance to the RHD. The NMCP will train health workers on IPTp, ensure that the delivery of IPTp services at health facilities follows directly observed treatment (DOT), provide supportive supervision, and implement M&E, OR, and BCC campaigns related to MIP at the community level. A policy for community level IPTp has not been developed. Village Health Teams, which work at the community level, will mobilize pregnant women to attend all visits at ANC clinics. The RHD is now responsible for IPTp implementation, and activities are integrated within the FANC policy and procedures. A well-functioning national MIP TWG, which includes the RHD and NMCP, has been established and meets regularly to coordinate and discuss MIP-related issues.

In addition to case management, pregnant women received ITNs as part of the universal coverage campaign completed in 2014, and will continue to receive ITNs through routine distribution at ANC clinics. According to the 2014 MIS, 75% of pregnant women slept under an ITN the night preceding the survey, increasing significantly from 44% in 2009.

---

[9]Updated WHO Policy Recommendation (October 2012); Intermittent Preventive Treatment of malaria in pregnancy using Sulfadoxine-Pyrimethamine (IPTp-SP)

Since 2006, PMI has supported the development of a comprehensive MIP training module that was incorporated into the FANC training. PMI has also supported the training and on-the-job supervision of over 10,084 health workers on IPTp. Additionally, it has provided job aids such as pregnancy wall charts and gestational wheels in all facilities providing antenatal care, and PMI has supported the adoption of a MoH nationwide advocacy plan for IPTp. PMI has purchased and distributed 171,033 and 107,270 SP treatments, respectively, since the start of PMI for use in PNFP facilities. In collaboration with PEPFAR, PMI has focused on integrating IPTp services with prevention of mother-to-child transmission (PMTCT) and extended this support to private health facilities. PMI continued to provide safe water and drinking cups for DOT. As a result of these efforts, the percentage of pregnant women receiving two doses of IPTp has increased to 60% by 2012 in the regions covered by PMI, according to HMIS data and an implementing partner's final report. Antenatal attendance by pregnant women in Uganda remains high, with 2011 DHS results showing that 94% of pregnant women made at least one ANC visit, and 48% made four or more visits. However, only 21% of women made their first ANC visit before the fourth month of pregnancy and the IPTp2 uptake was low despite the various efforts undertaken by PMI and other partners.

The 2014 MIS revealed that the IPTp2 uptake in Uganda has increased from 25% (DHS 2011) to 45%. Even though the progress made is significant, with an increase of 20% within three years, this still falls short of the PMI target of 85%. In addition, IPTp3 coverage in Uganda is low, recorded at 25% in the 2014 MIS. With high antenatal attendance for at least one ANC visit, many opportunities for the provision of IPTp are being missed in Uganda.

Multiple hypotheses have attempted to explain the low coverage rates of IPTp including unwillingness of some pregnant women to take SP because they are not aware of the need for malaria prevention in pregnancy. Some women also fear SP could have side effects on the fetus, a fear sometimes fostered by health workers.[10] Low IPTp uptake may also be attributed to negligence of midwives not giving SP to pregnant women, SP stockouts, and irregular ANC attendance by pregnant women.[11] Malaria Consortium completed a study in 2014 that assessed the barriers to IPTp uptake in Uganda. The research concluded that, despite a range of minor concerns (for example with regard to taking IPTp on an empty stomach), women and communities have largely positive views of ANC and IPTp. Refusal rates of IPTp are low and given the high ANC attendance figures, the main obstacles to the provision of IPTp are therefore likely to be supply-side challenges.[12] In the past, many health facilities struggled with frequent stockouts of the drug used for IPTp, although this has been improving as MoH provides all SP to meet

---

[10]Barker J, Payes R, (2007). "Overview of Programmatic Interventions for Communication for Indoor Residual Spraying (IRS), Insecticide-treated Nets (ITNs), Case Management and Malaria in Pregnancy." USAID.

[11]Ndyomugyenyi R and Katamanywa J. 2010. Intermittent preventive treatment of malaria in pregnancy (IPTp): do frequent antenatal care visits ensure access and compliance to IPTp in Ugandan rural communities? *Trans R Soc Trop Med Hyg*

[12]Assessing and addressing barriers to IPTp uptake in Uganda by malaria consortium 2015

the nationwide need in the public sector. Private facilities on the other hand have to buy their own supplies, which mean stockouts are still a problem. Another major barrier to the provision of IPTp is health workers' inadequate knowledge with regard to when and how to provide IPTp. This is compounded by the incoherent and outdated information that existed at the time in many policy documents and job aids that are supposed to guide health workers. Moreover, the policies in use at that time were not in line with the most recent WHO policy recommendations for the provision of IPTp; these policies have since been updated.

Based on the findings of the survey and the PMI team's field observations, together with substantial support from PMI, the NMCP successfully mobilized adequate resources and coordinated stakeholders to update the national MIP policy, guidelines, manuals, job aids, and BCC materials. In addition, the HMIS was updated to collect data on uptake of three or more doses of IPTp. All relevant documents were updated and enriched through workshops and submitted to the senior MoH leadership for their endorsement, which is imminent. Now that the policy has been endorsed, PMI will support dissemination of these materials and training of health workers on the new policy.

Progress during the last 12–18 months

PMI supported integrated support supervision (ISS) on IPTp to strengthen health workers' knowledge and skills, including interpersonal communication of health workers with clients and DOT. In PMI focus districts, 71% of health facilities were reached with ISS and had at least two health workers trained in the IPTp quality improvement approach. PMI supported the training of 579 health workers on IPTp in 2014.

PMI has also supported quarterly monitoring of SP stock levels in health facilities to maintain adequate supplies for IPTp. Stock results were shared with the NMCP to encourage the replenishment of low stocks at the National Medical Stores (NMS). PMI supported on-the-job mentorship of health workers and DOT to help increase IPTp2 uptake. PMI continued to help make clean drinking water available for IPTp use in 30 target districts.

In collaboration with PEPFAR, PMI has supported integrating IPTp within other HIV prevention efforts such as PMTCT services. This support has also been extended to PNFP health facilities. PMI also supported the integration of MIP activities within district-based efforts aimed at strengthening FANC.

Commodity gap analysis

Table 6: SP Gap Analysis for MIP

Calendar Year	2015	2016	2017
Total population	35,800,000	36,831,040	37,891,774
SP Needs			
Total number of pregnant women attending ANC*	1,432,000	1,437,242	1,515,671
Total SP Need (in treatments)**	**4,296,000**	**4,311,726**	**4,547,013**
Partner Contributions			
SP carried over (deficit) from previous year	0	0	0
SP from MoH	4,296,000	4,311,726	4,547,013
SP from Global Fund	0	0	0
SP from other donors	0	0	0
SP planned with PMI funding	0	0	0
Total SP Available	**4,296,000**	**4,311,726**	**4,547,013**
Total SP Surplus (Gap)	**0**	**0**	**0**

Assuming 80% of all pregnant women will attend ANC.
**Assuming three treatments per pregnant woman.
***The Government of Uganda is committed to procuring and distributing the total amount of SP doses required for each year (2015-2017).

Plans and justification

With FY 2016 funds, PMI will continue to provide assistance in strengthening the MoH's capacity to coordinate and implement MIP programs, including supporting the implementation of the revised MIP policies. There will also be a renewed focus on strengthening health worker performance related to MIP as a comprehensive component of FANC services. This includes making trainings more geographically accessible for health workers, providing supportive supervision specifically for MIP, and integrating trainings on other infectious diseases such as HIV. PMI will continue to advocate for minimizing missed opportunities and increasing the availability of MIP services. With FY 2016 funds, PMI will continue strengthening the delivery of MIP services, thus increasing IPTp uptake in both the public and private sector. PMI will work with the NMCP to coordinate and bring onboard all RBM partners in country to implement the feasible recommendations of the 2014 IPTp barriers study to overcome the factors contributing to low IPTp uptake.

New MIP guidelines were adopted by the MoH/NMCP. PMI will support the NMCP to: 1) disseminate the updated MIP documents and train health workers according to WHO recommendations; 2) advocate for, coordinate, and ensure that 0.4mg folic acid, and 30-60mg iron are procured and distributed; and 3) promote the new iron and folic acid doses for daily use by pregnant women at ANC clinics.

The MoH will procure and distribute the required quantity of SP for 2015, 2016, and 2017. Iron and folate are also included in the MoH's supply of essential medicines.

Proposed activities with FY 2016 funding: ($652,500)

- **Strengthen delivery of comprehensive IPTp services as part of an integrated FANC approach at public and PNFP ANC clinics:** PMI will continue to support the NMCP and DHMTs in the implementation of the new IPTp policy; address factors contributing to low IPTp uptake; train newly recruited health workers; distribute clean water and cups to facilitate DOT of IPTp; enhance BCC to ensure pregnant women understand that taking three or more doses of IPTp is safe; and encourage pregnant women to utilize the ANC services available to them. PMI will support the distribution of ITNs and IPTp, as well as early diagnosis and prompt treatment of MIP. PMI will also assist with ISS for ANC health workers with an emphasis on IPTp, ITNs, and case management of pregnant women. PMI will continue supporting professional associations to improve the level of communication between ANC providers (midwives, nurses, and doctors) and their clients during ANC visits. PMI will also support integrating service delivery with other treatments such as PMTCT. Furthermore, PMI will support the NMCP to: 1) disseminate the MIP updated documents and train health workers according to WHO recommendations; 2) advocate for, coordinate, and ensure that 0.4mg folic acid, and 30-60mg iron are procured and distributed; and 3) promote the new iron and folic acid doses for daily use by pregnant women at ANC clinics. ($552,500)
- **Support for comprehensive IPTp services for ANC in private-for-profit (PFP) health facilities:** A considerable number of pregnant women use PFP health facilities due to better service delivery and geographic location. PMI will continue to promote IPTp by training health workers in small- to medium-sized PFP health facilities in order to promote a comprehensive package of IPTp services. These services will include DOT, early detection of MIP, and encourage regular reporting of the services provided. PMI also seeks to leverage ongoing support from PEPFAR and MCH funds for the private sector. ($100,000)
- **BCC**: *See cross-cutting BCC section for details on activities and funding.*

4. Case management

a. Diagnosis and Treatment

NMCP/PMI objectives

The UMRSP recommends parasitological diagnosis and prompt treatment with ACTs to reduce malaria-related morbidity and mortality. Parasite-based diagnosis with microscopy or RDTs is prioritized in all health facilities and at the community level through iCCM for all age groups. However, approximately 60% of people with fever cases seek treatment from any private provider including drug shops, vendors, and medicine sellers that are not registered and do not report through the HMIS system. According to estimates from the 2014 HMIS, of people with fever who sought treatment from registered and reporting health facilities, 85.6% used government-owned facilities, 8.6% used PNFP health facilities, and 2.5% used PFP health facilities. In 2010, Uganda adopted an iCCM strategy that indicates that two of the five VHT members are responsible for diagnosis and treatment of common childhood illnesses, including malaria.

The strategy calls for:
- All suspected malaria cases to be subjected to parasite-based diagnosis.
- Microscopy to remain the "reference or gold standard" for malaria diagnosis in case management and to be the diagnostic method of choice for all HC III's (that have microscopes) and above.
- RDTs to be used at HC III's that do not have microscopes, all HC II's, at the community level, and to fill the gaps at higher level HCs where microscopy is not possible.
- The type of RDT to be deployed in Uganda to be guided by evidence on sensitivity, specificity, ease of use, and stability in the field, as determined by the performance evaluation and pre-qualification schemes of the WHO coupled with in-country testing. Multiple RDT brands are allowed according to this national policy.
- iCCM to be rolled out to all villages across the country in a phased manner to facilitate access to and reduce the treatment gap for malaria, pneumonia, and diarrhea.
- The Test, Treat, and Track initiative to be rapidly scaled up to ensure early detection and appropriate treatment, and to promote good surveillance for accurate reporting of cases.
- Supportive supervision and clinical audits to be strengthened to improve adherence to policies and guidelines.
- Referral systems from lower level HCs, the community, and the private sector to be strengthened to improve management of severe malaria.

Overall, this policy is consistent with WHO guidance on the need for parasitological confirmation of fevers in all groups before treatment with antimalarial drugs.[13] Even though improvements in malaria diagnostic practices have been made, adherence to the policy is suboptimal with most malaria diagnosis still based on clinical symptoms. The UMRSP objective for diagnostics by 2018 is to ensure at least 90% of malaria cases in the public and private sectors and at the community level receive prompt diagnosis and treatment according to national policy, however, field observations during site visits and facility record reviews suggest limited practice by either health workers or patients to request testing prior to treatment or to adhere to testing results. This challenge has been further exacerbated by the lack of adequate laboratory diagnostic capacity, especially the inadequate number of laboratory technicians in many health facilities. Consistent with the field observations of diagnostic practices, the 2014 MIS found that only 36% of children with a fever were tested for malaria before receiving treatment. Future efforts will require ongoing education of health workers and other cadres of health staff to base

---

[13]WHO. 2015. Guidelines for the treatment of malaria –3rd edition.

treatment on parasitological test results, and to educate communities to request a malaria test as a component of good medical care for fever.

The responsibility for the coordination, monitoring, and supervision of all HC III and IV laboratories resides with the Central Public Health Laboratory (CPHL). The CPHL is grossly understaffed resulting in irregular supervision and limited ability to improve laboratory performance for malaria diagnostics, in particular quality assurance of microscopy. PMI and PEPFAR will continue their collaboration in laboratory strengthening by supporting the CPHL and the NMCP to conduct regular supervision of facilities for sustained quality diagnostic services.

The UMRSP also plans for a phased rollout of iCCM to all villages across the country, emphasizing support for a consistent supply of malaria commodities, to improve prompt and correct malaria diagnosis and treatment at the community level. This policy is in line with WHO and UNICEF recommendations that countries implement iCCM for children less than five years of age as an essential method for improving access to malaria diagnosis and treatment. The iCCM approach provides diagnosis and treatment of pneumonia, diarrhea, and malaria through VHTs using standard algorithms. It also provides a platform for facilitating referral of severe illness, including the use of pre-referral rectal artesunate.

In line with WHO recommendations and as a means for ensuring that the national policy for the recommended first-line drugs are appropriate, the UMRSP provides strategic guidance for studies to routinely monitor ACT efficacy. Current first-line drugs for uncomplicated malaria are artesunate/amodiaquine (AS/AQ) and artemether-lumefantrine (AL), while the second-line is dihydroartemisinin-piperaquine (DP). However, it is important to note that DP is frequently used in the private sector. Injectable artesunate is the drug of choice for treatment of severe malaria.

Progress since PMI was launched

PMI has invested in the training and supervision of health workers on malaria diagnosis and treatment, procurement of RDTs and ACTs, and drug quality testing to improve malaria case management in Uganda. Over the last six years, PMI has supported the training of over 40,000 health workers in malaria diagnosis and treatment. On average, over 85% of public and PNFPs have benefited from PMI supported training for case management. This figure includes health workers who have received training 3-4 times in case management due to changes in malaria diagnosis and treatment policies, high turnover of staff, and required refresher training. In FY 2012, PMI supported the rollout and use of RDTs in health facilities without laboratory services, microscopy training at health facilities with laboratory services, and both types of training to facilities with limited laboratory services. In the last six years, PMI has purchased over 3.9 million RDTs. Although PMI support for commodities has included both the public and PNFP sectors in previous years, currently USG-supported RDTs and ACTs are only permitted through the PNFP distribution mechanism, the Joint Medical Stores.

Since 2006, over 6.2 million ACT treatments were purchased by PMI. Starting in 2011, PMI supported training of private health practitioners in the revised (2010) antimalarial drug policy. This training is often integrated with sessions on HIV/AIDS, family planning, and child survival. To date, nearly 35,000 health practitioners have received training in malaria treatment. In addition, PMI has supported small-to-medium sized private clinics and has worked with large private corporations to leverage additional funds for malaria control through their corporate social responsibility programs. These corporations provide free or subsidized health services to their employees and surrounding communities. PMI works with these businesses on a cost-sharing basis for ITNs, IPTp, and laboratory diagnostics. Refresher trainings in case management and diagnostics are also provided by the NMCP with support from PMI and clinical audit approaches have been adopted to promote high quality and operational efficiency at all levels of health service provision. Even though there is still a considerable amount of work to be done to improve quality of care for patients with malaria, PMI has been addressing these weaknesses through implementation of supportive supervision, clinical audits, and training.

To address not only the availability of malaria diagnostics but the quality of diagnostic tests, in particular microscopy, PMI has supported the development and implementation of quality assurance procedures. In 2012, the quality and validity of the malaria slides stained and read at the sentinel sites was assessed. Based on the findings, PMI supported the shift of the malaria staining technique from Field stain to Giemsa stain at all surveillance sites. This shift allowed for quality assurance measures by allowing re-readings of slides kept over time. A monthly slide rechecking program was also introduced at all of the sites to help monitor the quality of preparation and accuracy of reading smears. As a result, the majority of the sites scored above 85% for sensitivity, specificity, and percentage agreement. Technical support for QA activities for diagnostics previously consisted of: conducting microscopy training and follow-up, testing retention of proficiency achieved after training, developing the RDT and the microscopy QA manual, and working with the national program to officially approve these QA programs. Although there was progress made in development of the QA program, implementation was limited because of the lack of ability to finalize the policy document at the national level. Moving forward, PMI will support QA activities in health facilities, and ensure that QA of diagnostic services are scaled-up.

Uganda has monitored first-line antimalarials since 2001, and PMI has supported this work since 2006. As of 2009, evidence showed that all formulations of ACTs tested were still highly efficacious in Uganda.[14,15] Studies conducted in 2006 and 2009 have compared AL, AS/AQ, and DP. The most recent therapeutic efficacy study from 2014 comparing AS/AQ and AL found that both ACT regimens were highly efficacious in treating uncomplicated malaria. To improve access to diagnosis and treatment of

---

[14]The Four Artemisinin-Based Combinations (4ABC) Study Group (2011) *A Head-to-Head Comparison of Four Artemisinin-Based Combinations for Treating Uncomplicated Malaria in African Children: A Randomized Trial.* PLoS Med 8(11): e1001119. doi:10.1371/journal.pmed.1001119

[15]Emmanuel Arinaitwe,Taylor G. Sandison Humphrey Wanzira, Abel Kakuru, Jaco Homsy, Julius Kalamya, Moses R. Kamya,Neil Vora,Bryan Greenhouse, Philip J. Rosenthal, Jordan Tappero, and Grant Dorsey. *"Artemether-Lumefantrine versus Dihydroartemisinin-Piperaquine for Falciparum Malaria: A Longitudinal, Randomized Trial in Young Ugandan Children,"* Clinical Infectious Diseases 2009; 49:1629–37

malaria, Uganda has developed considerable experience in using iCCM. With funds from donors, Uganda has been able to demonstrate the feasibility of iCCM in the Mid-West and Central regions with an estimated population of about five million people. However, and despite the great promise shown by iCCM in increasing health coverage especially for children living in remote areas, iCCM scale-up in other regions has been slow, partly due to the uncertainty of funds.

The NMCP has a case management TWG which meets regularly as a valuable forum for technical experts to: a) discuss key issues that support the NMCP in expanding access to effective treatment, b) monitor the implementation of case management strategies and methods for scaling up, c) identify and document best practices from studies in case management within and outside Uganda, d) disseminate information and implementation updates, and e) identify key scale-up gaps and priorities for action. The working group consists of members from the NMCP, PMI, DFID, CHAI, Malaria Consortium, UNICEF, WHO and other malaria stakeholders. The availability of RDTs, ACTs, laboratory supplies, and trained staff at all levels are also discussed and actions are taken accordingly.

Progress during the last 12–18 months

PMI supported the NMCP to improve the capacity of health workers in diagnosis and treatment of malaria over the past 12-18 months. In addition, PMI supported the NMCP to update the country's guidelines for diagnosis with microscopy and RDTs. Notably, these guidelines specifically recognize the necessity of supporting both the public and private sector, in order to increase the proportion of suspected malaria cases receiving testing prior to treatment. The guidelines also recommend that Giemsa stain is used for malaria microscopy in all facilities. These national parasite-based diagnosis implementation guidelines are currently being reviewed at the senior management level for approval.

In FY 2014, PMI supported the training of 893 health workers in malaria diagnostic testing. As a precursor to the trainings, PMI supported the NMCP in the development of the training curriculum for IMM which included: 1) management of both uncomplicated and severe malaria (with proper administration of IV artesunate); 2) management of MIP; and 3) parasite-based diagnosis with RDTs, including how to manage a patient with a negative RDT and fever. The results of these IMM trainings showed a significant increase in knowledge and skills among health workers. Subsequent supervision visits were used to reassess diagnostic competence, provide on-the-job training, and allow the NMCP to collect data on how the trainings affected the overall management of fever cases.

In FY 2014, PMI procured 762,150 ACT treatments and 655,000 artesunate injections. In addition, PMI trained nearly 2,047 health facility workers in treatment of malaria with ACTs. PMI did not procure RDTs in FY 2014 because of the availability of RDTs from the Global Fund for distribution through the PNFPs that PMI would have supported. Commodity supply to public sector health facilities remains a major challenge. The Mission has serious issues with the NMS' capacity, accountability, and transparency and will not currently provide malaria and non-malaria USG-procured commodities (PEPFAR, SMGL, RH/FP, and others) to the NMS. This chronic problem can be resolved if the capacity, accountability, and transparency of the NMS are improved. For USG-procured commodities to go through the NMS, a major transformation process within the NMS and the MoH is needed. These exercises will need high level advocacy, budgetary, and system support from the GoU. Until the issue is resolved with the NMS, PMI advocates for commodities to reach the public sector through the JMS in hard-to-reach areas and in times of outbreaks. However, the Global Fund continues to distribute commodities through the NMS. PMI will support high level efforts to resolve the above-mentioned issues with the NMS. Areas of focus will also include installing a web-based ordering system, harmonized coding of malaria commodities, procurement planning, and budget tracking.

As part of PMI's goal to leverage and coordinate with other malaria donors, PMI provided technical assistance to the NMCP during the development of their Global Fund concept note for the New Funding Model in 2014. The approved iCCM funding from the Global Fund will cover 33 districts — 15 in 2015 and 18 in 2016 (contingent upon sufficient progress). PMI also assisted the NMCP in updating its national iCCM policy, training materials, and development of guidelines for the rollout of iCCM. The policy and the training materials are expected to be available by September 2015.

PMI with WHO supported a randomized, single-blinded trial in three sites comparing the efficacy and safety of AS/AQ and AL for the treatment of uncomplicated malaria in children between 6 and 59 months in Uganda; patients were enrolled in a 28-day study from May 2013 to June 2014, and a comprehensive analysis has recently been completed. Both regimens were effective with no early treatment failures, were well tolerated, and had few side effects; however AS/AQ was associated with a decreased risk of parasite recurrence over 28 days of follow-up.[16] Full results, including *P. falciparum* genetic polymorphisms testing, should be presented and published in late 2015.

Poor management of severe cases appears to be a leading cause of deaths due to malaria in Uganda. PMI is currently supporting a project to improve case management of severe malaria in children by implementing a training package and measuring changes in case management practices. Results should be available mid-2016.

---

[16] tesunate/amodiaquine versus artemether/lumefantrine for the treatment of uncomplicated malaria in Uganda: a randomized trial Adoke Yeka, Ruth Kigozi, Melissa Conrad, Myers Lugemwa, Peter Okui, Charles Katureebe

Commodity gap analysis

Table 7: RDT Gap Analysis

Calendar Year	2015	2016	2017
RDT Needs			
Target population at risk for malaria	35,800,000	36,831,040	37,891,774
Total number projected fever cases [I]	60,944,905	63,054,230	65,224,152
Health service coverage in Uganda	80%	85%	90%
Total number of fever cases that can access services	48,755,924	53,596,096	58,701,737
Percent of fever cases confirmed with microscopy	25%	24%	19%
Percent of fever cases confirmed with RDT	75%	76%	81%
Total RDT Needs[*]	**36,566,943**	**40,733,033**	**47,548,407**
Partner Contributions			
RDTs carried over (deficit) from previous year	0	0	0
RDTs from MoH	0	0	0
RDTs from Global Fund [II]	17,136,947	19,530,711	0
RDTs from other donors[III]	1,458,615	286,614	0
RDTs planned with PMI funding	8,153,846	2,346,154	3,307,692[IV]
Total RDTs Available	**26,749,408**	**22,163,479**	**3,307,692**
Total RDT Surplus (Gap)	**(9,817,535)**	**(18,569,554)**	**(44,240,715)**

NB: all data obtained from country quantification exercise
[I] *Fever cases are based on morbidity data extrapolated from consumption data from the HMIS per age category.*
[II] *Current Global Fund grant ends December 31, 2016; however, the subsequent grant is expected to supply malaria commodities for 2017*
[III] *Support from other donors in 2017 is unknown at this time*
[IV] *These commodities will be procured using previous years' existing funds, not FY 2016 funds*
[*] *Total national RDT needs includes public, PNFP, PFP, and iCCM (community) needs*

Table 8: ACT Gap Analysis

Calendar Year	2015	2016	2017
ACT Needs			
Target population at risk for malaria	35,800,000	36,831,040	37,891,774
Total number projected fever cases [I]	60,944,905	63,054,230	65,224,152
Health service coverage in Uganda	80.0%	85.0%	90.0%
Total number of fever cases that can access services	48,755,924	53,596,096	58,701,737
Estimated fever cases to be positive by RDTs and microscope	85.0%	85.0%	85.0%
Total ACT Needs	**41,442,535**	**45,556,682**	**49,896,476**
Partner Contributions			
ACTs carried over (deficit) from previous year	3,240,120	0	0
ACTs from MoH	1,571,885	1,571,885	1,571,885
ACTs from Global Fund [II]	10,674,729	15,968,197	0
ACTs from other donors[III]	922,430	894,345	0
ACTs planned with PMI funding	1,034,482	1,137,931	1,137,931[IV]
Total ACTs Available	**17,443,646**	**19,572,358**	**2,709,816**
Total ACT Surplus (Gap)	**(23,998,889)**	**(25,984,324)**	**(47,186,660)**

NB: all data obtained from country quantification exercise

[I] Fever cases are based on morbidity data extrapolated from consumption data from the HMIS per age category.

[II]Current Global Fund grant ends December 31, 2016; however, the subsequent grant is expected to supply malaria commodities for 2017

[III] Support from other donors in 2017 is unknown at this time

[IV] These commodities will be procured using previous years' existing funds, not FY 2016 funds

Plans and justification

PMI and the NMCP will work closely with WHO to support the scale-up of an appropriate QA/QC system for diagnostics and continue to support strengthening treatment for uncomplicated and severe malaria through training, supportive supervision, clinical audits and on-the-job mentoring. This will be done in both the public and private facilities. PMI support will complement Global Fund and PEFPAR funding for general laboratory and microscopy strengthening and will continue working with PEPFAR to coordinate USG efforts to improve the laboratory system in Uganda. PMI will also work with the Global Fund to coordinate the procurement of malaria supplies and commodities (including RDTs and ACTs) to be distributed to PNFP facilities through the JMS. PMI will prioritize strengthening clinical services in communities via iCCM in four Central and North West districts and at health facilities, including the procurement of RDTs and ACTs using existing funds from previous years.

There are current plans to evaluate the efficacy and safety of AL and DP (commonly used in the private sector) for treatment of uncomplicated malaria in children in Uganda. The results will inform stakeholders in the region of the current level of efficacy of AL and DP. Given the recent findings with AS/AQ, PMI plans to include all three drugs in future testing.

Of recent concern is a new molecular marker for artemisinin resistance found on the Kelch gene on chromosome 13 (K13). This resistance is now reported in the entire Mekong region including Cambodia, Thailand, Vietnam, Laos, and Myanmar and more recently near the Indian-Myanmar border. However, the K13 molecular marker has only been shown to be associated with slow clearance in South East Asia. Additional studies have found mutations in the K13 gene in Africa, but it is not yet clear if those new mutations are associated with slow clearance. Nevertheless it is important to assess the prevalence and the spread of those mutations, as artemisinin resistance has been shown to have emerged independently in different places. Uganda will therefore seek to be included in a core-funded study covering several other countries.

In addition, PMI will implement clinical audits, focusing on facilities at all levels with the highest volume of patients, ensuring that commodities are available in PMI-supported facilities, and using updated outpatient registers. PMI will also work to tailor the current integrated management of malaria (IMM) for the health facility level, and focus more on fever management than malaria management, which should improve quality of care, and increase testing compliance. At the community level, expanding iCCM efforts should improve access to care, and shorten the time between symptoms, testing, and treatment.

Proposed activities with FY 2016 funding: ($3,990,000)

- **Support QA/QC and supportive supervision for diagnostics at health centers:** PMI will support case management trainings that focus on appropriate diagnosis, QA/QC (including slide bank development used for proficiency testing, regular slide rechecking, and consideration for RDT QA/QC using new technology as it becomes standardized and approved), and supportive supervision for diagnostics in approximately 70% of the districts in the country. Three regionally focused mechanisms are needed given the Mission's integrated health service approach. These three mechanisms will implement the same package of malaria interventions and will cover different geographical areas (central, eastern, east-central, south-west, mid-west, north, and west Nile districts), which when combined provide close to national coverage. ($1,300,000)
- **Support improved diagnostics in the for-profit private sector:** PMI will support training on the use of RDTs, supervision, and quality assurance (for both RDTs and microscopy) in the for-profit corporate private sector through existing partnerships with 55 companies through the 1:1 matching contribution program for malaria (18 participating companies currently). ($160,000)

- **Strengthen case management in public health facilities:** PMI will provide funds for strengthening treatment of uncomplicated and severe malaria in public and PNFP health facilities in most of parts of Uganda. This support includes clinical audits, supportive supervision, pre and in-service training, iCCM in four districts, provision of job aids to health workers, enhancing collaboration between NMCP and the national professional councils (doctors, nurses, midwives, laboratory technologists/technicians, and pharmacists). PMI will also provide funds for strengthening collaboration between district health teams and district-level professional associations to promote correct diagnosis, and early and prompt treatment. Health care workers who are new to the system, practice in areas with a high burden of malaria, and/or who have shown poor performance will be prioritized. ($2,000,000)
- **Support private sector providers and their networks to strengthen malaria treatment and increase the role of district health officials in providing support and supervision:** PMI will continue supporting private clinics and drug shops that are the closest sources of care for children with fever in many communities. This support includes enhancing collaboration between the public sector district health teams and private sector associations to ensure that health workers and drug shop owners receive routine supportive supervision for proper clinical care of children with fever, including treatment based on parasitological diagnosis, and support improvements in record-keeping and HMIS reporting to the national level. ($250,000)
- **Monitor drug resistance (efficacy) of antimalarial drugs:** Drug efficacy studies have traditionally been conducted every two years but will shift to alternating two to three sites every year, and FY 2016 funds will be used to study AS/AQ, AL, and DP. ($250,000)
- **TDYs from CDC/Atlanta:** With three TDYs, CDC staff will provide technical support for laboratory diagnostics scale-up and QA/QC policy implementation and technical support for quality of care issues for the management of severe and uncomplicated malaria within PMI and NMCP programs. ($30,000)

b. Pharmaceutical Management

NMCP/PMI objectives

The UMRSP provides strategic guidance to strengthen the NMCP's capacity for procurement and supply chain management of malaria commodities; as quantification of malaria commodities is a primary role of the Quantification and Planning Unit in the Pharmacy Division of the MoH. The NMCP and the district health teams conduct integrated supervision and inspection of the supply and distribution process in the public, private, and PNFP sectors. The NMS and JMS procure and distribute these commodities to all levels of care through both the 'pull' and 'push' basic kit system. However, commodity supply to public sector health facilities remains a major challenge. Serious concerns have been raised about the NMS' capacity, accountability, and transparency. Therefore, malaria and non-malaria USG-procured commodities (PEPFAR, SMGL, RH/FP, and other) are not being supplied to the NMS.The NMS manages the procurement and distribution of essential medicines and health supplies for the public sector from other donors, including the Global Fund, while JMS manages similar activities for the PFP and PNFP sector. PMI will continue to distribute malaria commodities to PNFP facilities through the JMS until the challenges with the NMS are resolved.

Progress since PMI was launched

Together with PEPFAR and other USG health programs, PMI has strengthened the national pharmaceutical management system by improving performance and financial management, clarifying pharmaceutical policy, and increasing the transparency of the logistics management information system. However, improvements are still needed, especially in the supply of ACTs and other commodities to districts and lower level health facilities.

National ACT supplies have been more stable in the last four years due to procurements from the Global Fund, DFID, and the GoU. The 'push' kit introduced by the MoH and NMS three years ago has helped to improve stock levels of ACTs routinely available at all lower level public health facilities. The 'push' kit, however, does not take into account the actual needs of individual health facilities, thus some facilities have stockouts while others have overstock. Efforts have been made by the districts, MoH, and PMI partners to redistribute supplies in these cases as well as document the under- and over-supply of ACTs to assist the central commodity store in revising the contents of the kits.

Quality of antimalarial drugs is a concern worldwide. Uganda's National Drug Authority (NDA) conducts quality control at ports of entry as well as post-marketing surveillance. Multiple partners provide support including the Global Fund and PMI through a wider USAID partnership.

Progress during the last 12–18 months

PMI provides technical assistance to the NMCP, district health teams, and facilities to improve the supply chain management and develop accurate stock inventories of AL, RDTs, SP, and severe malaria drugs. Progress has been seen in the past 12–18 months in ensuring stable supplies of malaria commodities at health facilities and improving stock management and reporting. PMI supported an end-use verification (EUV) survey in 75 randomly selected health facilities in 15 districts to assess the performance of the public health supply chain, focusing on malaria commodities. The activity provided information regarding the availability of malaria commodities, as well as insight into how malaria is being managed at the health facility level. The findings were analyzed and a report shared in late 2014. Results from the EUV survey indicated: 1) low coverage of IMM training suggesting that health workers are not updated about changes in the NMCP malaria case management policy, 2) low testing rate despite high stocks of RDTs found at health facilities, 3) adequate availability of ACTs at health facilities sampled with 87 percent of facilities having ACTs available in at least one pack size. The EUV recommended regular health worker training and supervision, operational research to understand why health workers still prescribed ACTs to patients that tested negative for malaria, and the development of an open-source cost-effective electronic data collection system to ease data entry and analysis. Recommendations will be used to make programmatic improvements and address problems with product availability through the current supply chain activity.

Plans and justification

PMI will continue to support the NMCP in strengthening the NDA through an integrated health sector program that focuses on improving their strategy and capability in information management as well as their quality control and inspection programs. PMI will distribute malaria commodities through JMS until the efforts of the mission toward addressing the challenges with NMS get resolved.

Proposed activities with FY 2016 funding: ($300,000)

- **Strengthen pharmaceutical supply chain management and monitor drug quality of antimalarials**: PMI will continue to provide technical assistance to the NMCP/MoH to forecast national requirements for essential medicines, and coordinate national supply planning among the various suppliers. Malaria-specific activities will include: forecasting and quantification of malaria commodity needs including ACTs, SP, RDTs, and other antimalarial medicines; reporting on these commodities when distributed to the PNFP sector; and supporting monitoring of ACT stockouts in all facilities. PMI will work with the JMS to continue monitoring and improving the ordering and distribution system for PMI-procured ACTs and RDTs. In addition, technical assistance will be provided to the district and health facility levels to strengthen the lower level supply chain system. PMI in collaboration with the Global Fund and DFID will provide support to the NDA to improve their quality control activities for priority and high-risk medicines, including antimalarials, that are supplied to the country. The PMI investment in supply chain management leverages more than $5 million from other health funding streams (including PEPFAR) to strengthen the entire supply chain system. ($300,000)

5. Health system strengthening and capacity building

PMI supports a broad array of health system strengthening activities which cut across intervention areas, such as health workforce strengthening including supportive supervision, supply chain management and health information systems strengthening, drug quality monitoring, and NMCP capacity building.

NMCP/PMI objectives

Health system strengthening is a key component of Uganda's health sector strategic plan 2011–2015. PMI support covers four components: 1) improved health workforce development and management; 2) improved infrastructure of existing health facilities with emphasis on providing minimum quality standards of health care services, especially in the areas of maternal and child health through (a) renovation of selected health facilities, (b) provision of medical equipment, (c) improved capacity for operations and maintenance, and (d) strengthening the referral system; 3) improved leadership, management, and accountability for health service delivery; and 4) improved maternal, newborn and family planning services through improving access to, and quality of, maternal health, newborn care, and family planning services.

Progress since PMI was launched

Over the last several years, PMI has provided over $6 million to complement the efforts of other USG programs supported by USAID, CDC, PEPFAR, and the GoU. PMI provides support to heath system strengthening through its implementing partners and the integrated USAID/Uganda health system approach. In collaboration with PEPFAR and other USAID health programs, PMI supports improvement in workforce policy, planning, and management through: 1) strengthening human resource units and information systems in the ministries of health, education, and sports, in health professional councils, and in districts; 2) development and implementation of evidence-based human resources strategies; 3) advocating for increased funding and support for health workforce that increased staffing levels, retention and productivity; and 4) developing in-service and pre-service training plans.

Capacity building of the NMCP has been continuously supported by the two PMI senior technical advisors and two malaria program management specialists on all aspects of malaria control activities and programming. These advisors have played key roles in the country's malaria technical working groups, RBM partners' forums, and coordination taskforces. Since 2008, PMI has also equipped the NMCP with computers and accessories, scanners, and photocopiers.

As part of the wider health system, the private sector continues to play an important role in the delivery of health services in Uganda, with more than 60% of the population seeking care from the private sector as their first point of entry into the health system[17]. PMI has been supporting the private sector and increased private sector involvement in malaria control and has engaged at least 15 major corporations that invested their own funds to provide malaria services to both their workers and surrounding communities. PMI has also provided malaria commodities to PNFPs.

Progress during the last 12–18 months

PMI supported the NMCP to strengthen coordination with malaria stakeholders through RBM forums, technical working groups, malaria scientific sessions, review meetings, assessments (capacity and VHTs) and surveys (e.g., MIS 2014), the impact evaluation (2000–2011), and review of policies, guidelines, manuals, and job aids (e.g., MIP). PMI provided technical assistance to revitalize five major technical working groups focused on M&E, IVM, case management, MIP, and BCC. PMI also supported the USAID/Uganda sector-wide initiative to address human resource shortages and develop the capacity of the health workforce at national and district levels.

PMI supported the NMCP to recruit two fellows under CDC's Public Health Fellows Program (PHFP) / Field Epidemiology and Training Program (FETP). This program offers training for the fellows in

---

[17]Uganda National Household Survey 2006, Ministry of Health

epidemiology and disease outbreak investigation. One fellow supports the NMCP's M&E unit and the second fellow supports multiple malaria activities, including coordinating with partners and districts at the subnational level.

As malaria surveillance sites have transitioned to reference centers, there has been an increasing emphasis on improving case management, data management, surveillance and reporting at the health facility, district, and national levels using GoU personnel, thus greatly increasing the sustainability of these efforts.

Wherever practical, PMI has implemented malaria control activities together with other major health programs, particularly those for MCH, routine immunization, HIV/AIDS, tuberculosis, and other vector-borne diseases. PMI focused on the following areas:
- Strengthening health information systems
- Building leadership and technical capacity in the NMCP
- Linking and integrating malaria and MCH health services
- Supporting pharmaceutical and supply chain management
- Improving laboratory diagnostic services

Plans and justification

PMI will continue to support the capacity of the NMCP to manage and coordinate multi-sectoral malaria reduction efforts at all levels, including the continuation of regular NMCP technical and management meetings, RBM in-country partnership coordination meetings, and review and planning meetings. Beyond national coordination, PMI will continue to support FETP, Peace Corps, and human resource development and management. PMI will also work with the NMCP to conduct an assessment and develop a long-term strategy for Uganda's enhanced surveillance sites to determine how this PMI investment can best contribute to improving surveillance capacity in Uganda.

In collaboration with PEPFAR and other USG health programs, PMI will continue to support regions and districts to improve health worker productivity, recruitment and retention, and staff training (pre-service and in-service). PMI will further engage the GoU to increase commitment, transparency, and accountability for resources for malaria control and to mainstream malaria activities into the health sector response. To enhance the responsiveness of the health infrastructure and increase access to services, PMI will strengthen systems with expansion of VHT and iCCM in selected hard-to-reach areas.

PMI will continue supporting the USAID/Uganda sector-wide initiative to address human resource shortages and develop the capacity of the health workforce at national and district levels. The evaluation of this initiative pointed to the need to enhance the performance of the health workforce in terms of quality health care provision and productivity. Therefore, the strengthening human resources for health activity will develop and support performance-based financing, strengthen leadership and management, and harness private sector pre-service training capacity to meet priority human resources for health needs for malaria control. USAID/Uganda's district-based programs will implement the human resources for health support package including leadership capacity development and performance management developed by the human resource initiative. PMI's investment leverages over $2 million of PEPFAR and other USG health investments for this area of health system strengthening. This activity will also include support for national MoH leadership training.

Furthermore, PMI will support updating of the curriculum for malaria case management in key institutions that train clinical staff. This will include each cadre of health workers potentially addressing malaria (doctors, clinical officers, different levels of nurses, midwives). Once the curriculum is developed, it will be incorporated in the education curriculum in schools across Uganda. PMI also plans to support a platform for health teaching staff to share notes in formal and informal forums across both public and private health worker training institutions to increase the body of knowledge and encourage uniformity in training and practice around malaria case management, which anecdotal reports have shown to be a gap in the country.

PMI will also support strengthening of national capacity for program planning, management, and monitoring through practical field placements of recent graduates in well-performing malaria programs where they can be mentored by experienced program managers in both GoU and NGO institutions. Through these placements, the graduates will receive on-the-job training. This initiative will fund at least four students to follow the malaria track in the two-year PHFP/FETP. In addition, PMI will continue to support three Peace Corps volunteers to conduct malaria awareness training and implement small malaria control projects in their communities.

Proposed activities with FY 2016 funding: ($980,000)

- **NMCP capacity building:** Capacity building support to the NMCP, RBM partnership support, coordination of partner meetings, and support to pre-service training through updating pre-service training curriculum to ensure that it reflects the updated malaria treatment guidelines and policies, and strengthening of a forum to share teaching notes across training institutions. ($150,000)
- **PHFP/FETP:** Four PHFP/FETP students to support the NMCP's program planning, management, M&E unit, and strengthening malaria surveillance at the national and subnational levels. ($300,000)
- **Strengthen human resources for health:** PMI will leverage PEPFAR resources in the strengthening of human resources for health project to support regions and districts to improve health worker productivity, recruitment and retention, and staff training (pre-service and in-service). The project will develop and support performance-based financing, strengthen leadership and management, and harness private sector pre-service training capacity to meet priority human resources for health needs for malaria control. The project will also support updating of the curriculum for malaria case management in key institutions that train clinical staff, and will include each cadre of health workers potentially addressing malaria (doctors, clinical officers, different levels of nurses, midwives). Human resources for health systems for improved health care quality and health workforce management practices at the NMCP, DHMTs,

and facility levels will be strengthened. PMI will support strengthening of overall national capacity for program planning, management and monitoring of health systems to improve malaria case management. ($500,000)

- **Peace Corps:** Support placement, training, and small-scale malaria projects for three Peace Corps volunteers and their counterparts at the community level. ($30,000)

Table 9: Health Systems Strengthening Activities

HSS Building Block	Technical Area	Description of Activity
Health Services	Case Management	Strengthen the quality of malaria diagnostic and treatment services through integrated management of malaria training, support supervision, and monitoring.
Health Workforce	Health Systems Strengthening	Build, through training and technical assistance, host country managerial and leadership capacity for effective malaria control.
Health Information	Monitoring and Evaluation	Strengthen malaria surveillance to guide PMI and NMCP decision-making, forecasting and program management; also, contribute to training and mentoring health facilities to improve data reporting using the new HMIS tools.
Essential Medical Products, Vaccines, and Technologies	Case Management	Support improved forecasting, procurement, quality control, storage and distribution of malaria commodities, such as insecticide-treated nets, artemisinin-based combination therapies, and rapid diagnostic tests.
Health Finance	Health Systems Strengthening	Provide technical assistance to leverage financial contributions and services from corporate private sector partners for for malaria prevention and control, e.g. extractive industries such as sugar and tea companies.
Leadership and Governance	Health Systems Strengthening	Strengthen national coordinating and regulatory bodies to direct and manage malaria resources, develop guidelines, and improve quality of services, and support a national forum for sharing teaching notes across health worker training institutions.

6. Behavior change communication

NMCP/PMI objectives

The UMRSP 2014–2020 calls for the NMCP to incorporate BCC into all malaria interventions to improve the access, appropriate use, and coverage at the community and household levels. The NMCP's main strategy for BCC is 1) to develop and implement national malaria BCC guidelines, 2) implement comprehensive BCC activities, and 3) monitor the impact of BCC interventions supported by the NMCP. The UMRSP also calls for the development of high quality communication materials for different communication platforms, identifying and engaging hard-to-reach populations, and improving advocacy for malaria control support in both the public and private sector. The strategy includes a target of at least 85% of the population to undertake correct practices in malaria prevention and treatment by 2017. In Uganda, funds that support malaria BCC come from the Global Fund, PMI, as well as other RBM partners.

Progress since PMI was launched

Past PMI-supported BCC activities have reached nearly all Ugandans with key malaria messages on the importance of net use, malaria testing, timely treatment, and prevention of malaria during pregnancy. PMI progress on BCC to date includes the development of the NMCP's national BCC strategy and training materials used by BCC implementing partners working in malaria prevention and treatment. Case management training for health workers and VHTs has included a BCC component and VHTs are given job aids and storyboards to conduct sensitization sessions on malaria prevention and treatment in their communities. The national BCC strategy, training materials and tools are used not only in the PMI target areas, but also by Global Fund implementers in the remaining areas of the country. PMI has also supported training of NGO staff on BCC related to malaria prevention, and supported Peace Corps volunteers to work with local NGOs on implementing malaria BCC activities in various districts.

Since 2006, PMI has provided support for the establishment and functioning of the national BCC TWG. The TWG was established in 2008 to coordinate BCC activities across partners, and is responsible for reviewing the technical content of all BCC messages pertaining to malaria, including the accuracy and harmonization of messages. The main audiences for focused PMI BCC programs have been beneficiary communities, opinion leaders, elders, pregnant women, children's caretakers, health workers, and drug dispensers.

Progress during the last 12–18 months

PMI supported BCC as a cross-cutting activity focusing on all interventions: case management, ITNs, and IPTp. In the past year, PMI supported the finalization of Uganda's national BCC strategy, which is now pending final MoH review. The strategy is based on the UMRSP and incorporates available technical evidence on BCC and findings of the midterm review. PMI included enhanced BCC in the nine current IRS districts focusing on IPC, radio, and IEC to encourage people to open their houses for spraying, continue to sleep under ITNs, and seek prompt diagnosis and treatment in the event of a fever. PMI activities continue to focus on key behaviors that need to be emphasized, e.g., regular use of ITNs and prompt diagnosis and treatment with ACTs for patients with fever. In the last 12–18 months, PMI supported the NMCP to reach approximately four million Ugandans with key messages around net use, care seeking behavior, and IPTp treatment through radio talk shows, school activities, and community mobilization through village health workers. Their outreach included 610 schools and approximately 484,000 schoolchildren.

PMI also supported a qualitative study of perceptions and practices related to mosquito net care and repair in two districts in eastern Uganda that found that net damage was common with the most cited causes being children and rodents. BCC in the country needs to continue to emphasize the importance of maintaining net integrity for malaria prevention purposes as well as for maintaining aesthetic appeal.

Preliminary results from the MIS 2014 show that, of women aged 15–49 years who had heard or seen a malaria message within six months before the survey, 82% got the message from radio and 34% from community health workers.

Plans and justification

PMI will continue to enhance BCC efforts for correct and consistent use of ITNs, increased IPTp uptake, acceptance of IRS where applicable and early diagnosis and treatment of malaria. With the shift of IRS to nine high burden eastern districts, PMI will continue enhancing BCC in the 10 northern districts from where IRS was withdrawn by promoting correct and consistent use of ITNs, IPTp uptake, and prompt malaria diagnosis and effective treatment. PMI will increase focus on interpersonal communication, encourage malaria messaging in PEPFAR programs, and ensure a strong BCC technical working group at the national level with the main focus to use BCC to drive down malaria prevalence in Uganda.

In addition, PMI will continue supporting targeted and evidence-based BCC interventions at the national, district, and community levels to increase ITN usage among children under five and pregnant women to reach the PMI target of 85%. PMI will continue to promote malaria prevention and treatment interventions for pregnant women, children under five, and households through community mobilization and mass media activities including integrated health outreach, radio talk shows, radio spots, community meetings, and interpersonal communication. These interventions will address existing barriers to uptake of malaria prevention and treatment services related to limited knowledge and skills and social and gender norms as well as target the interventions to get the right exposure and intensity required to achieve behavior change.

PMI will also continue supporting targeted community outreach in areas with high prevalence and low uptake of services and will print, distribute, and orient health workers and VHTs on the use of IPTp job aids and informational materials to increase demand and utilization of IPTp. Promotion of prompt care-seeking behaviors for suspected malaria, parasitological-based diagnosis, and appropriate treatment for those with confirmed malaria will also be emphasized. Focus will be placed on creating demand for diagnostics by health workers and patients, appropriate treatment, and adherence to prescribed treatment by health care providers. PMI will continue to support the test, treat, and track campaign to increase demand for testing for malaria followed by appropriate treatment. In addition, PMI will support effective communication on iCCM in districts where iCCM will be added. This activity will also leverage resources from the private sector.

PMI plans to support interpersonal communication (IPC) through community dialogues at community and household levels. PMI will also conduct enhanced BCC in the nine current IRS districts focusing on IPC, radio, and IEC to encourage people to open their houses for spraying, continue to sleep under ITNs, and seek prompt diagnosis and treatment in the event of a fever. In addition, PMI will continue to focus on additional community-based BCC in the former ten IRS districts. PMI will provide funding for malaria BCC activities while leveraging larger PEPFAR resources to fund malaria BCC activities at the national level.

Proposed activities with FY 2016 funding: ($800,000)

PMI BCC activities will continue to focus on key behaviors that need to be emphasized, e.g., regular use of ITNs and prompt diagnosis and treatment with ACTs for patients with fever, patient adherence to ACT treatment, and community IRS acceptance. Specific activities will include community IPC, radio, and other IEC activities through ANC clinics. Key activities are outlined below:
- Support comprehensive BCC for correct and consistent use and care of ITNs, increasing IPTp uptake, and improving early and accurate diagnosis of malaria at facility and community levels in 58 districts. ($400,000)
- Support BCC campaign in the private sector at district level to reinforce the role of small and medium private health providers; work through mass media and interpersonal communication to create demand for malaria prevention and treatment services; improve net use, and promote case management by providers in the iCCM districts. ($100,000)
- Increase adoption of healthy behaviors for malaria prevention and treatment through coordination, revision, and production of essential BCC materials for districts and strengthened health communication at the national level. ($300,000)

7. Monitoring and evaluation

NMCP/PMI objectives

The primary aim of the 2014 M&E Plan within the UMRSP is to provide a joint framework for a well-coordinated, systematic, and holistic tracking of progress in malaria control, informing refinement and guiding decision-making for program improvement. The goals of the plan are to: a) describe the types of data and data sources, and how data will flow from the primary source to a central repository through appropriate decision making layers, and to all relevant stakeholders; b) provide a framework for the collection, processing, reporting, analysis and use of malaria data in Uganda; c) provide standard indicators, targets and frequency of reporting in a standardized format for all malaria implementers and stakeholders, d) guide the routine and periodic documentation of planned activities and measure expected outputs, outcomes and impact; and e) define implementation arrangements with clear responsibility centers.

Progress since PMI was launched

PMI has supported the use of the following tools to measure malaria burden as a result of ongoing control and prevention efforts:
- 2010 Anemia and Parasitemia Survey: This survey provided information on anemia and parasitemia in children under five years of age and district-level coverage data in two districts with and without IRS in northern Uganda, with similar distribution of ITNs and case management support.
- 2011 ITN Coverage Survey: This survey provided information on net coverage at district levels in the central region of Uganda after the targeted mass ITN distribution campaign in early 2010.
- 2011 Uganda DHS: The DHS provided data comparable to the 2006 DHS which assessed anemia levels in children under five years of age.

PMI-supported malaria surveillance sites were established in different malaria transmission zones in 2006 in six outpatient centers and in 2010 in six hospitals, providing high quality longitudinal data. To increase the representativeness of valid malaria case numbers captured at health facilities, the outpatient sites were used as the basis for outreach surveillance capacity building in a number of health center IVs in select epidemiologically relevant districts. These 26 facilities were labeled as malaria reference centers, and were provided with additional resources and supervision to ensure high levels of testing for suspected cases and adherence to test results. These centers collect data with the newly enhanced outpatient register. The NMCP and partners, including PMI, use the data to understand the burden of malaria in the catchment areas served by these facilities and how the burden has been changing with intervention scale-up. Malaria cases reported from the surveillance system are laboratory-confirmed and are considered valid and reliable. This information is crucial for interpreting the malaria case numbers from facilities. In addition to central level use for programmatic decision-making and dissemination, such as the 2000–2011 Impact Evaluation, the data are used at multiple levels of the health system and by malaria partners for planning and tracking progress of interventions towards malaria control. The data from surveillance sites have positively impacted case management practices by health workers at health center IVs and hospitals through regular monitoring and data dissemination workshops. A robust quality control system for microscopists has been initiated and the results indicate excellent performance in accuracy of blood slide readings across all sites.

Progress during the last 12–18 months

2014 Malaria Indicator Survey (MIS)
PMI worked with the NMCP and other partners to organize stakeholder meetings, determine methodology, and raise additional funds for the MIS to meet the targeted season for better and reliable results. Efforts were made to ensure comparability with the previous MIS (2009) and DHS (2011). The

MIS 2014 provided data on the status of net ownership and use after the UCC among children under five years of age and pregnant women, as well as IPTp uptake in ANCs. Through oversampling the 10 previous IRS districts in the north and the 14 new IRS districts in the east, the MIS demonstrated the impact of IRS in the north, and provided a pre-spray baseline for the new IRS districts. Preliminary results were made available to all malaria stakeholders and the general public in April 2015 for World Malaria Day.

Impact Evaluation 2000–2011
From 2000 to 2011, the under-five mortality dropped by 41% in Uganda. During the same time period, Uganda made substantial progress toward implementing malaria control interventions, particularly distribution of ITNs, IRS, and IPTp for prevention and ACTs for case management. The Uganda RBM Impact Evaluation measured the changes in malaria morbidity and mortality following scale-up of malaria control interventions, particularly for the period 2000–2011, taking into account the implementation of other child survival programs. The results showed that malaria interventions plausibly contributed to the reduction of mortality among children under five years of age during this time period. Of note is that the largest part of the scale-up corresponded to the biggest drop in the under-five mortality (2006–2011).

HMIS
PMI assisted the NMCP and the MoH's Resource Center to update HMIS data collection forms to match PMI's enhanced surveillance (to include fever, malaria test results, and treatment). This will greatly improve the system to collect and report standardized malaria-related indicators once the forms are disseminated. Data from private facilities remains largely absent from the HMIS, and efforts by PMI partners continue to include data quality support at district-level private facilities. Currently, the district health information system 2 (DHIS2) covers all districts in Uganda. HMIS reports are entered at district level for onward submission to the headquarters. Text-based data collected at facility level (through the mTrac system), as well as data from the 32 PMI-supported enhanced surveillance sites, now feed directly into the DHIS2.

Data use
In May 2015, the ninth quarterly Malaria Bulletin for Uganda was published and disseminated to key stakeholders. The Malaria Bulletin has proved to be a useful tool for reviewing malaria data reported through HMIS and the surveillance network, and has been well received by the RBM partners at the international, national, and district levels. The additional support from the PHFP/FETP to assist with data review and publication of the quarterly bulletin has helped the NMCP with key M&E activities. Another PHFP/FETP project is to map HMIS data (incidence and test positivity rates) for the MoH to better visualize data, especially for monitoring trends over time in order to better direct public health resources. The national M&E TWG has been meeting monthly, with regular participation from NMCP, PMI, and partners, to discuss issues; these meetings inform the NMCP Program Manager, the Resource Center, and the quarterly RBM meetings. However, additional staff is needed to make better use of improved malaria surveillance data for programmatic decision-making as well as donor reporting. A

functional malaria database could help the NMCP store, analyze, and make use of malaria data from HMIS, supply chain systems, intervention activities, and partners.

Enhanced surveillance
In 2014 PMI established 26 sustainable outpatient surveillance reference centers. Six of the reference centers were established at previous outpatient surveillance sites and the other 20 were established at new sites. New reference centers were strategically located to monitor the malaria burden in districts that are targeted for a change in intervention coverage—specifically, this includes reference centers in districts with former, current, or possible future IRS or iCCM. Thus far, surveillance data from these sites has been used to monitor the effect of a universal net campaign, to evaluate the effect of a shifting IRS strategy, and to make evidence-based decisions in the face of an epidemic. PMI will build on the success of the reference centers to continue to strengthen HMIS/DHIS2 data collection and analysis at facility, district and national levels. These reference centers are in addition to the six inpatient sites which collect data on malaria cases and malaria case management practices in hospitals, and also feed directly into HMIS/DHIS2. PMI will work with the NMCP to conduct an assessment and develop a long-term strategy for Uganda's enhanced surveillance sites to determine how this PMI investment can best contribute to improving surveillance capacity in Uganda.

Strengthening the capacity of the Vector Control Division (VCD)
PMI has assisted the NMCP/Vector Control Division (VCD) at central and district levels to build local entomologic capacity. Production of susceptible *Anopheles gambiae* Kisumu strain mosquitoes from insectaries in Gulu, VCD, and Tororo continues to support IRS QA and monthly insecticide decay monitoring. Insecticide susceptibility assays of malaria mosquitoes occur nationwide on an annual basis at six sentinel sites to determine resistance status to WHO-approved IRS insecticides and to monitor for changes in resistance status. Insecticide intensity assay training (monitoring for operation impact of resistance) and synergist bioassays to detect for the presence of oxidative enzymes in malaria mosquitoes (used to detoxify pyrethroid insecticides) was taught to 15 vector control officers and conducted in four IRS monitoring sites in June (2015). The entomology branch in Atlanta identified *An. gambiae* complex mosquitoes collected from northern Uganda with PCR to monitor the composition of *An. gambiae/An. arabiensis* in IRS districts.

Implementing partner monitoring and evaluation
PMI contributes to a USAID/Uganda Mission-wide data collection mechanism for all implementing partners. This project assists partners in developing performance management plans, collecting and tracking data on key program indicators and conducting data quality assessments. This project provides continuous external monitoring and evaluation of all Mission projects.

End-use verification study
PMI, working with the NMCP, supported an EUV study in early 2015. The EUV was conducted in 15 districts sampled from across the country. Results from the study indicated a 13-point reduction in the percentage of OPD cases that are attributed to malaria from 36% in the 2014 EUV compared to 23% in the 2015 EUV. The survey also indicated a low testing rate of 61 percent despite high RDT availability,

which was at 93% on the day of the visit. In addition, the survey also found that 81% of negative under-five cases were still given ACTs on the day of the survey, indicating that a large proportion of negative test patients are still treated for malaria. Further, the study found that at least one ACT pack was available on the day of the survey indicating that although pack sizes varied from facility to facility, patients could still be treated with an ACT. The study recommended enhanced support supervision, mentorship, and training of health workers on integrated management of malaria and additional BCC. PMI/Uganda plans to incorporate these recommendations into the implementation of the new TBD malaria flagship project, the ongoing national BCC mechanism, and upcoming integrated health programs currently in design.

Improving case management of severe malaria in children
Ongoing monitoring activity on case management for severe malaria is expected to promote evidence-based best practices for malaria case management, facilitate timely identification and management of children with severe malaria, and strengthen the organizational capacity of hospitals to improve the availability of basic, yet essential, commodities required for the management of severe malaria in children.

Table 10: Monitoring and Evaluation Data Sources

Data Source	Survey Activities	Calendar Year								
		2010	2011	2012	2013	2014	2015	2016	2017	2018
National-level Household surveys	Demographic Health Survey (DHS)		X					(X)		
	Malaria Indicator Survey (MIS)					X				(X)
Health Facility and Other Surveys	EUV survey	X	X			X	(X)	(X)	(X)	(X)
Malaria Surveillance and Routine System Support	Support to malaria surveillance system	X	X	X	X	X	X	(X)	(X)	(X)
	Support to HMIS	X	X	X	X	X	X	(X)	(X)	(X)
Therapeutic Efficacy monitoring	In vivo efficacy testing		X		X	X		(X)	(X)	(X)
Entomology	Entomological surveillance and resistance monitoring		X	X	X	X	X	(X)	(X)	(X)
Other malaria-related evaluations	Northern Uganda Anemia and Parasitemia study				X					
Other Data Sources	Malaria Impact Evaluation					X				

Plans and justification

PMI support will focus on collecting high quality, complete, and timely malaria data using HMIS/DHIS2 for public, PNFP, and PFP facilities. There are challenges in collecting data from a number of PFP facilities as there are no updated records either at central or district levels to locate and identify the PFP facilities, as they frequently change their names and locations. It has been reported by the Resource Center of the MoH that small and medium level PFP facilities are reluctant to report. However, PMI in collaboration with RBM partners will continue to support the Resource Center to update its database on PFP facilities. PMI funds will also support training of the persons involved in collection and analysis of malaria data at the subnational and health facility levels, as well as supportive supervision and data audits for malaria focal persons at the regional and district levels, and district biostatisticians to strengthen HMIS/DHIS2 to include data from PFP as well. The district health management team is responsible for monitoring data collection, and analyzing and reporting data for all health facilities including PFP and PNFP facilities.

Uganda's M&E plan with FY 2016 funds will focus on:
- Continuing support to build malaria surveillance capacity through sentinel sites, malaria reference centers, and existing health facilities
- Ensuring all surveillance efforts are coordinated and data are fed into the NMCP's M&E unit to be used for decision-making and reporting
- Continuing support for the quarterly malaria bulletin, the national malaria M&E TWG, and M&E activities at a sub-national level
- Utilizing malaria surveillance capacity to monitor changes in malaria burden as intervention strategies are changed
- Monitoring the effectiveness of existing interventions through
  - net durability monitoring
  - insecticide resistance monitoring

Proposed activities with FY 2016 funding: ($2,175,000)

- **Support malaria surveillance network:** As a part of the malaria surveillance network strategy, all 26 of the existing outpatient malaria reference centers will continue to improve case management practices (including testing compliance rates), and serve as a technical resource for surrounding facilities. They also serve as a platform for drug monitoring studies. The six inpatient sites will continue to collect data on malaria cases and malaria case management practices in hospitals, and PMI will continue to share the data with the NMCP to better monitor and improve management of severe malaria. PMI will also work with partners to continue to decrease the cost per site. Malaria case surveillance will be enhanced in at least one health center in every IRS district. PMI will continue to encourage non-malaria stakeholders to leverage reference centers for their own surveillance and studies. ($575,000)
- **Program monitoring and tracking system development at subnational level**: PMI will continue to support the HMIS at subnational and health facility levels, in coordination with the overall USG support from USAID, PEPFAR, and CDC. With FY 2016 funding, PMI support will focus on collecting complete, accurate, and timely malaria data for public, PNFP and PFP facilities with HMIS/DHIS2, using the enhanced malaria surveillance as a model. PMI funds will also support training of the persons involved in collection and analysis of malaria data at the subnational and health facility levels, as well as supportive supervision and data audits for malaria focal persons at the regional and district levels, and for district biostatisticians. ($630,000)
- **Program monitoring and tracking system development at the national level:** PMI will continue to support the M&E unit at the NMCP and the HMIS/DHIS2 systems related to malaria to improve their capacity for data collection, analysis, and reporting. PMI will also continue to

support and actively participate in the NMCP's M&E TWG to ensure coordination of data collection across partners. PMI in collaboration with RBM partners will support the Resource Center to update its database on PNFP and PFP facilities. ($100,000)

- **Entomologic surveillance:** PMI will continue to build local entomologic capacity by assisting the NMCP/Vector Control Division (VCD) at central and district levels. Production of susceptible *Anopheles gambiae* Kisumu strain mosquitoes from insectaries in Gulu, VCD, and Tororo will support IRS QA and monthly insecticide decay monitoring. Insecticide susceptibility assays of malaria mosquitoes will occur nationwide on an annual basis at six sentinel sites to determine resistance status to WHO-approved IRS insecticides and to monitor for changes in resistance status. Four districts (two IRS, one IRS-withdrawn, and one never sprayed) will be assayed twice a year for resistance to monitor the impact of IRS insecticide use and to determine the type and presence of metabolic resistance using CDC synergist bioassays (once yearly). CDC bottle bioassay technique and training will be provided along with WHO tube bioassays and district vector control officers will be engaged where assays are conducted. CDC bottle intensity assays and training will occur in the same four districts to measure operational impact of resistance to IRS and ITNs. Comprehensive vector surveillance and bionomics studies will occur at two sites in each of three districts (two IRS, one IRS-withdrawn) and will include indoor/outdoor biting preference, hourly biting activity, indoor density determinations with pyrethrum spray collections, and CDC light trap collections for species composition and identification with PCR. Malaria case surveillance will be enhanced in at least one health center in every IRS district. FY 2016 funds will support training, field costs, and procurement of equipment, supplies, laboratory maintenance, and sample analysis. ($600,000)
- **PMI data collection and reporting**: PMI will continue to support the USAID/Uganda Mission-wide M&E Project that serves as the central data collection point for all implementing partners. ($50,000)
- **ITN longevity:** PMI will support the ongoing prospective ITN monitoring study that includes: 1) estimations of net survivorship/attrition and physical integrity, 2) measuring bioefficacy using cone bioassays, and 3) measuring hole development over time.($100,000).
- **End-use verification**: PMI will continue to conduct EUV surveys annually in 75 randomly selected health facilities in ten districts to determine the availability of antimalarials at the end user level and how effective supply chain systems are used in managing malaria commodities. The EUV surveys provide useful data on supply chain management and malaria case management, which can be used to strengthen the health care system through informed decision-making. ($100,000)
- **Two TDYs from CDC/Atlanta**: CDC staff will provide technical support for M&E activities including the HMIS and malaria reference centers. Two visits are planned to ensure adequate follow up of planned activities. ($20,000)

8. Operational research

NMCP/PMI objectives

Operational research is included within the NMCP's national M&E plan, with a focus on therapeutic efficacy testing and insecticide susceptibility studies. PMI continues to support OR as part of the new PMI Strategy for 2015–2020. Objectives include:

- Improving effectiveness and scale-up of existing interventions, including assessing combined interventions (e.g., ITNs and IRS);
- Evaluating ways to mitigate insecticide and drug resistance; identifying and assessing improved and cost-effective approaches to monitoring changes in malaria burden;
- Identifying and assessing approaches to improve the capacity of health systems to better deliver malaria interventions;
- Assessing new interventions that offer the potential for use by PMI-supported programs in the near future; and
- Assisting in optimizing program efficiency by addressing bottlenecks in malaria prevention and control.

Progress since PMI was launched

Since becoming a PMI focus country in 2006, Uganda has been involved in various OR studies that have helped inform malaria prevention and control programmatic policies. Prior to 2006, Uganda was implementing a home-based malaria treatment package, called Homapak, consisting of a combination of choloroquine and SP. The package was distributed through community drug distributors for treatment of fever in children under five within 24 hours of onset at home. With the change to AL as the first-line treatment for malaria, PMI supported a study to evaluate the process of rolling out community ACTs in one district. Results showed that there were some problems with the change in treatment schedule for AL and issues surrounding packaging for age groups. As a result, PMI supported the scale-up of supportive training and supervision and comprehensive monitoring of drug distributions.

Early OR done in Uganda on verbal autopsy was influential in PMI's decision to no longer use verbal autopsies to determine malaria-specific mortality. In 2007, PMI supported a prospective study to examine the validity of verbal autopsies for determining deaths due to malaria in children under five in three different epidemiological settings in Uganda. The cause of death was compared using results of a verbal autopsy survey (a follow-on to the 2006 DHS), and the "gold standard" of health facility medical records. Results showed the sensitivity of verbal autopsy procedures were variable. Sensitivity was 63% (95% CI: 46-80) in the high transmission setting of Tororo and 57% (95% CI: 43-71) in the medium transmission setting of Kampala. Specificity was high at both sites (89% and 90%, respectively). The positive predictive value for verbal autopsies was very different in Tororo and Kampala (83% vs 34%; difference 49% [95% CI: 31-67], p<0.001). In the low transmission setting of Kisoro, no deaths were attributable to malaria on review of the medical records. These results reiterated that verbal autopsies are not useful for all settings, and should not be used to determine malaria-specific mortality within acceptable bounds.

A PMI-core funded study was completed in 2011 to evaluate the effectiveness of a post-campaign door-to-door hang-up and communication intervention to increase net usage. The three-arm study compared net hang-up and utilization after 1) two visits to households by a village health team; 2) three visits to households by a village health team; and 3) no visits. All three study arms showed increase in net deployment from 56-63% at baseline to 67-74% at follow-up. Likewise, the three arms showed increases in the proportion of household members sleeping under the net the previous night of the follow-up survey. However, there was no statistical effect of household visits post-campaign on the hang-up or use of nets.

Progress during the last 12–18 months

During the past 12–18 months, a core-funded PMI study was conducted to understand the knowledge, attitudes, beliefs, and practices that motivate or impede net care and repair behaviors and to use these finding to inform a BCC intervention. The evaluation showed that the BCC program resulted in improved knowledge and attitudes of respondents, which impacted positively on net condition. This was likely the result of overall better care for the nets, as repairing did not contribute to improved net condition.

Although delayed due to Institutional Review Board approval, a study protocol and data collection forms have been developed for the operational research project to estimate the effectiveness of the collaborative improvement (CI) approach to improve the quality of routine malaria surveillance data. The proposed intervention will begin in mid-2015 and will include two components: 1) provide in-service training to health facility staff on collecting and reporting malaria surveillance data; and 2) implement the collaborative improvement approach via training and ongoing coaching for health facility staff on quality improvement methods and "learning sessions". Given the timing and delay of the study, assessments will be made after one or two rounds of implementation of the CI approach. Expected outcomes include: 1) malaria control intervention stakeholders having a generalizable knowledge of the key barriers to quality malaria health facility-based data, and how CI can be used to improve the quality of malaria data reported through HMIS; 2) added insight into how the CI process works and identification of determinants of successful implementation of the CI approach; 3) higher quality health facility data reported through the HMIS, resulting in increased data usage by health facility workers and decision-makers.

Uganda's malaria epidemiology is undergoing rapid changes as effective interventions are scaled up. The preliminary results of MIS 2014 show an enormous reduction of malaria prevalence among children under five years of age compared to the 2009 MIS, and provide an opportunity to understand the impact of malaria interventions. In addition, having country-specific data on durability and bioefficacy of ITNs will inform future mass ITN campaigns in Uganda. The NMCP in 2014 restarted the Uganda Malaria Research Centre (UMRC), but to date it still suffers from a lack of organization and funding. PMI and partners will continue to work with the NMCP and the UMRC to develop a prioritized OR list for Uganda.

Table 11: PMI-funded Operational Research Studies

Completed OR Studies			
Title	**Start date**	**End date**	**Budget**
Home-based management of fever	2007	2007	$100,000
Validation of verbal autopsies	2007	2007	$300,000
Effectiveness of post-campaign door-to-door hang-up and communication interventions to increase ITN utilization	12/2010	07/2011	$230,000
Net Care and Repair Behaviors: Formative Research in Uganda	03/2013	04/2014	$175,000
Ongoing OR Studies	**Start date**	**End date**	**Budget**
Title			
Improving the quality of health facility data to monitor trends in malaria burden: Effectiveness of the Improvement Collaborative Approach	05/2015	09/2015	$500,000
Planned OR Studies FY 2016			
Title	**Start date (est.)**	**End date (est.)**	**Budget**
No planned studies for FY 2016			

Plans and justification

No operational research studies are planned with FY 2016 funding.

9. Staffing and administration

Two health professionals serve as resident advisors to oversee PMI in Uganda, one representing CDC and one representing USAID. In addition, three Foreign Service Nationals (FSNs) work as part of the PMI team. All PMI staff members are part of a single interagency team led by the USAID Mission Director or his/her designee in country. The PMI team shares responsibility for development and implementation of PMI strategies and work plans, coordination with national authorities, managing collaborating agencies and supervising day-to-day activities. Candidates for resident advisor positions (whether initial hires or replacements) will be evaluated and/or interviewed jointly by USAID and CDC, and both agencies will be involved in hiring decisions, with the final decision made by the individual agency.

The PMI professional staff work together to oversee all technical and administrative aspects of PMI, including finalizing details of the project design, implementing malaria prevention and treatment activities, monitoring and evaluation of outcomes and impact, reporting of results, and providing guidance to PMI partners.

The PMI lead in country is the USAID Mission Director. The day-to-day lead for PMI is delegated to the USAID Health Office Director and thus the two PMI resident advisors, one from USAID and one from CDC, report to the USAID Health Office Director for day-to-day leadership, and work together as a part of a single interagency team. The technical expertise housed in Atlanta and Washington guides PMI programmatic efforts.

The two PMI resident advisors are based within the USAID health office and are expected to spend approximately half their time sitting with and providing technical assistance to the national malaria control programs and partners.

Locally-hired staff to support PMI activities either in Ministries or in USAID will be approved by the USAID Mission Director. Because of the need to adhere to specific country policies and USAID accounting regulations, any transfer of PMI funds directly to Ministries or host governments will need to be approved by the USAID Mission Director and Controller, in addition to the U.S. Global Malaria Coordinator.

Proposed activities with FY 2016 funding: ($2,209,916)

- **CDC staffing and administration**: Management costs and CDC resident advisor's salary. ($550,000)
- **USAID staffing and administration**: Management and administration costs, USAID resident advisor and three FSN salaries, CDC and USAID resident advisors' ICASS costs, and 2% program development and learning costs. ($1,659,916)

Table 1: Budget Breakdown by Mechanism

President's Malaria Initiative – Uganda
Planned Malaria Obligations for FY 2016

Mechanism	Geographic Area	Activity	Budget ($)	%
TBD/Supply Chain Contract	National	Procure ITNs	7,110,126	21.55%
TBD/MAPD	Central, mid-west and north west (west Nile)	Mixed distribution of ITNs through multiple outlets; strengthen delivery of comprehensive IPTp services as part of integrated FANC at ANC; support QA/QC and supportive supervision for diagnostics at health centers; strengthen case management in public sector; monitor drug resistance (efficacy) of antimalarial drugs; NMCP capacity building; comprehensive BCC for ITNs, IPTp, and early and accurate diagnosis of malaria; support malaria surveillance network; program monitoring and tracking system development at subnational and national level; support the prospective ITN monitoring study	6,174,458	18.71%
TBD/Regional health projects	East, East Central, South West	Routine ITN distribution through ANC/EPI services; strengthen delivery of comprehensive IPTp services as part of integrated FANC at ANC; support QA/QC and supportive supervision for diagnostics at health centers; strengthen case management in public sector; program monitoring and tracking system development at subnational level	1,511,000	4.58%

TBD/Northern regional health project	Northern	Routine ITN distribution through ANC/EPI services; strengthen delivery of comprehensive IPTp services as part of integrated FANC at ANC; support QA/QC and supportive supervision for diagnostics at health centers; strengthen case management in public sector; comprehensive BCC for ITNs, IPTp, and early and accurate diagnosis of malaria; program monitoring and tracking system development at subnational level	762,000	2.31%
Abt Associates/IRS project	Eastern, East Central	One round of spraying with OP in nine high burden districts, develop local capacity to expand and sustain IRS, and entomological surveillance.	12,943,500	39.22%
TBD/Social marketing project	National	Support for comprehensive IPTp services in private sector; support private sector providers and their networks to strengthen malaria treatment and increase the role of district health officials in providing support and supervision; BCC campaign at district level	450,000	1.36%
Cardno Emerging Markets/PHS Project	East Central	Support improved diagnostics in the private sector	160,000	0.48%
Management Sciences for Health/UHSC	National	Strengthen pharmaceutical supply chain management and end-use verification	400,000	1.21%
Peace Corps	National	Support placement, training, and small scale malaria projects for Peace Corps volunteers and their counterparts at the community level.	30,000	0.09%
FHI 360/ Communication for Health Commodities	National	Production of essential BCC materials for districts and strengthen health communication at the national level	300,000	0.91%
QED LLC/the learning contract	National	PMI data collection and reporting	50,000	0.15%

Intrahealth/SH RH	National	Strengthening HRH systems for improved health care quality and health workforce management practices at NMCP, DHMTs and facility levels.	500,000	1.52%
CDC IAA	National	Procure insecticide resistance monitoring supplies, insectary support (equipment and supplies) and PCR reagents as needed; 7 TDYs to provide TA for planning, implementation of IRS and monitoring of vector control, case management and M&E activities; in-country staffing and administration; and 4 FETP students	949,000	2.88%
USAID		In-country staffing and administration	1,659,916	5.03%
Total			**33,000,000**	**100%**

Table 2: Budget Breakdown by Activity

President's Malaria Initiative – Uganda
Planned Malaria Obligations for FY 2016

Proposed Activity	Mechanism	Budget Total $	Budget Commodity $	Geographic Area	Description
			PREVENTIVE ACTIVITIES		
Insecticide-treated Nets					
Procurement of ITNs	TBD/Supply Chain Contract	7,110,126	7,110,126	National	Procurement of 1,991,632 ITNs (1.4 million for delivery through continuous distribution channels and 591,632 for the universal coverage campaign).
Mixed distribution of ITNs through multiple outlets	TBD/MAPD	2,089,958	0	National	For distribution of 591,632 ITNs for the 2016/2017 universal coverage campaign, 550,000 ITNs for distribution in ANC and EPI and 600,000 ITNs for distribution in schools, which will be used as outreach distribution points in hard-to-reach areas.
Routine ITN distribution through ANC/EPI services	TBD/Regional health projects	210,000	0	East, East Central, South West	Routine distribution of 175,000 free ITNs to pregnant women and caregivers at ANC and EPI visits respectively.
Routine ITN distribution through ANC/EPI services	TBD/Northern regional health project	90,000	0	Northern	Routine distribution of 75,000 free ITNs to pregnant women and caregivers at ANC and EPI visits respectively.
SUBTOTAL ITNs		9,500,084	7,110,126		

71

Indoor Residual Spraying					
Support IRS	Abt Associates	12,243,500	8,600,000	Eastern, East Central	One round of spraying with OP in nine high burden districts to protect approximately 3 million people in the Eastern and East Central regions.
Develop local capacity to expand and sustain IRS	Abt Associates	100,000	0	National	Continue to use the available private sector opportunities in Uganda to support widespread, evidence-based IRS through effective partnership with the private sector in collaboration with MoH/NMCP.
Entomology equipment and supplies	CDC IAA	20,000	20,000	National	Procure insecticide resistance monitoring supplies, insectary support (equipment and supplies) and PCR reagents as needed.
Technical assistance	CDC IAA	29,000	0	National	Two technical assistance visits for planning and monitoring IRS activities, including testing for resistance mechanisms, training in CDC bottle intensity assays, mosquito surveillance and resistance training.
SUBTOTAL IRS		12,392,500	8,620,000		
Malaria in Pregnancy					
Strengthen delivery of comprehensive IPTp services as part of integrated FANC at ANC	TBD/MAPD	419,500	0	43 high burden districts	Support NMCP and DHMTs in the implementation of the new IPTp policy guidelines; address factors in the low IPTp uptake; train health workers; and encourage pregnant women to utilize ANC available ANC services. Support distribution of ITNs and IPTp.
Strengthen delivery of comprehensive IPTp services as part of integrated FANC at ANC	TBD/Northern regional health project	32,000	0	Northern	Support NMCP and DHMTs in the implementation of the new IPTp policy guidelines; address factors in the low IPTp uptake; train health workers; and encourage pregnant women to utilize ANC available ANC services. Support distribution of ITNs and IPTp.

Activity	Mechanism	Budget	Budget	Geographic Focus	Description
Strengthen delivery of comprehensive IPTp services as part of integrated FANC at ANC	TBD/Regional health projects	101,000	0	East, East Central, South West	Support NMCP and DHMTs in the implementation of the new IPTp policy guidelines; address factors in the low IPTp uptake; train health workers; and encourage pregnant women to utilize ANC available ANC services. Support distribution of ITNs and IPTp.
Support for comprehensive IPTp services in private sector	TBD/Social marketing project	100,000	0	Central, Mid West, North West	Promote IPTp by training of health workers in small- to medium-sized PFP health facilities in order to promote a comprehensive package of IPTp services.
Subtotal Malaria in Pregnancy		652,500	0		
SUBTOTAL PREVENTIVE		22,545,084	15,725,126		
			CASE MANAGEMENT		
Diagnosis and Treatment					
Support QA/QC and supportive supervision for diagnostics at health centers	TBD/MAPD	860,000	0	43 high burden districts	Support case management trainings that focus on appropriate diagnosis, QA/QC, and supportive supervision for diagnostics.
Support QA/QC and supportive supervision for diagnostics at health centers	TBD/Northern regional health project	140,000	0	Northern	Support case management training on appropriate diagnosis QA/QC, and supportive supervision for diagnostics.
Support QA/QC and supportive supervision for diagnostics at health centers	TBD/Regional health projects	300,000	0	East, East Central, South West	Support case management training on appropriate diagnosis, QA/QC and supportive supervision for diagnostics.
Support improved diagnostics in the private sector	Cardno Emerging Markets/PHS Project	160,000	0	East Central	Support training on the use of RDTs, supervision, and quality assurance in the for profit corporate private sector through existing partnerships

73

Activity	Project	Amount		Region	Description
Strengthen case management in public sector	TBD/MAPD	1,000,000	0	43 high burden districts	Strengthen treatment of uncomplicated and severe malaria in public, and PNFP health facilities, including clinical audits, supportive supervision, pre and in-service training, iCCM in four districts, provision of job aids to health workers, enhancing collaboration between NMCP and the national professional councils.
Strengthen case management in public sector	TBD/Northern regional health project	300,000	0	Northern	Strengthen treatment of uncomplicated and severe malaria in public, and PNFP health facilities, including clinical audits, supportive supervision, pre and in-service training, iCCM in four districts, provision of job aids to health workers, enhancing collaboration between NMCP and the national professional councils.
Strengthen case management in public sector	TBD/Regional health projects	700,000	0	East, East Central, South West	Strengthen treatment of uncomplicated and severe malaria in public, and PNFP health facilities, including clinical audits, supportive supervision, pre and in-service training, iCCM in four districts, provision of job aids to health workers, enhancing collaboration between NMCP and the national professional councils.
Support private sector providers and their networks to strengthen malaria treatment and increase the role of district health officials in providing support and supervision	TBD/Social marketing project	250,000	0	Central, Mid West, North West	Support private clinics and drug shops including enhanced collaboration between the public sector district health teams with the private sector associations to ensure that health workers and drug owners receive routine supportive supervision for proper clinical care of children with fever.

Activity	Mechanism	Coverage		Amount	Description
Monitor drug resistance (efficacy) of antimalarial drugs	TBD/MAPD	3 sites	0	250,000	Drug efficacy studies have traditionally been conducted every two years but will shift to alternating two to three sites every year, and FY 2016 funds will be used to study AS/AQ, AL, and DP, and include the new K13 testing with assistance from CDC, as well as genetic polymorphism testing.
Technical assistance	CDC IAA	National	0	30,000	Three technical assistance visits for laboratory diagnostics scale-up and QA/QC policy implementation and technical support to quality of care issues for the management of severe and uncomplicated malaria within PMI and NMCP programs.
Subtotal Diagnosis and Treatment			0	3,990,000	
Pharmaceutical Management					
Strengthen pharmaceutical supply chain management and monitor drug quality of antimalarials	MSH/UHSC	National	0	300,000	Provide technical assistance to the NMCP/MoH to forecast national requirements for essential medicines and coordinate national supply planning among the various suppliers.
Subtotal Pharmaceutical Management			0	300,000	
SUBTOTAL CASE MANAGEMENT			0	4,290,000	

HEALTH SYSTEM STRENGTHENING / CAPACITY BUILDING

75

NMCP capacity building	TBD/MAPD	150,000	0	National	Capacity building to NMCP, RBM partnership support, coordination of partners meetings and support to pre-service training through updating pre-service training curriculum to ensure that it reflects the updated malaria treatment guidelines and policies, and strengthening of a forum to share teaching notes across training institutions.
PHFP/FETP	CDC IAA	300,000	0	National	Four PHFP/FETP students to support the NMCP's program planning, management, M&E unit, and strengthening malaria surveillance at the national and subnational levels.
Strengthen human resources for health	Intrahealth/SHRH	500,000	0	National	Strengthening HRH systems for improved health care quality and health workforce management practices at NMCP, DHMTs and facility levels.
Peace Corps	Peace Corps	30,000	0	National	Support placement, training, and small scale malaria projects for three Peace Corps volunteers and their counterparts at the community level.
SUBTOTAL HSS & CAPACITY BUILDING		980,000	0		

BEHAVIOR CHANGE COMMUNICATION

Activity	Partner				Objective
Comprehensive BCC for ITNs, IPTp, and early and accurate diagnosis of malaria	TBD/MAPD	300,000	0	43 high burden districts	Support comprehensive BCC in correct and consistent use and care of ITNs, increasing IPTp uptake, and improving early and accurate diagnosis of malaria at facility and community levels.
Comprehensive BCC for ITNs, IPTp, and early and accurate diagnosis of malaria	TBD/Northern regional health project	100,000	0	Northern	Support comprehensive BCC in correct and consistent use and care of ITNs, increasing IPTp uptake, and improving early and accurate diagnosis of malaria at facility and community levels.
BCC campaign at district level	TBD/Social marketing project	100,000	0	National	Support BCC campaign at district level to reinforce the role of small and medium private health providers; work through mass media and interpersonal communication to create demand for malaria prevention and treatment services; improve net use, and promote case management by providers in the iCCM districts.
Production of essential BCC materials for districts and strengthen health communication at the national level	FHI 360/Communication for Health Commodities	300,000	0	National	Increase adoption of health behaviors for malaria prevention and treatment through strengthened health communication at the national level.
SUBTOTAL BCC		800,000	0		

MONITORING AND EVALUATION

Activity	Partner	Budget		Location	Description
Support malaria surveillance network	TBD/MAPD	575,000	0	National	The six inpatient sentinel sites will continue to collect high quality, in-depth data on malaria cases and case management practices and PMI will continue to share the data with the NMCP. New reference centers are strategically located to monitor the malaria burden in districts that are targeted for a change in intervention coverage. Malaria case surveillance will be enhanced in at least one health center in every IRS district.
Program monitoring and tracking system development at subnational level	TBD/MAPD	330,000	0	43 high burden districts	Support the HMIS at subnational and health facility levels, in coordination with the overall USG support from USAID, PEPFAR, and CDC, focusing on collecting high quality, complete, and timely malaria data using HMIS/DHIS2.
Program monitoring and tracking system development at subnational level	TBD/Northern regional health project	100,000	0	Northern	Support the HMIS at subnational and health facility levels, in coordination with the overall USG support from USAID, PEPFAR, and CDC, focusing on collecting high quality, complete, and timely malaria data using HMIS/DHIS2.
Program monitoring and tracking system development at subnational level	TBD/Regional health projects	200,000	0	East, East Central, South West	Support the HMIS at subnational and health facility levels, in coordination with the overall USG support from USAID, PEPFAR, and CDC, focusing on collecting high quality, complete, and timely malaria data using HMIS/DHIS2.
Program monitoring and tracking system development at the national level	TBD/MAPD	100,000	0	National	Support the M&E unit at the NMCP and the HMIS/DHIS2 systems related to malaria to improve their capacity for data collection, analysis, and reporting. Also support and actively participate in NMCP's M&E TWG to ensure coordination of data collection across partners.

Entomological surveillance	Abt Associates	600,000	0	National	Build local entomologic capacity by assisting the NMCP/Vector Control Division (VCD) at central and district levels. Insecticide susceptibility assays of malaria mosquitoes will occur nationwide on an annual basis at six sentinel sites to determine resistance status to WHO-approved IRS insecticides and to monitor for changes in resistance status.
PMI data collection and reporting	QED/the learning contract	50,000	0	National	Support the USAID/Uganda Mission-wide M&E Project that serves as the central data collection point for all implementing partners.
ITN longevity	TBD/MAPD	100,000	0	National	Support the third year of the prospective ITN monitoring study that includes: 1) estimations of net survivorship/attrition and physical integrity in two sites, 2) measuring bioefficacy using cone bioassays, and 3) measuring hole development through time.
End-Use Verification	MSH/UHSC	100,000	0	National	Conduct EUV surveys annually in 75 randomly selected health facilities in ten districts to determine the availability of antimalarials at the end user level and how effective supply chain systems are used in managing malaria commodities.
Technical assistance	CDC IAA	20,000	0		CDC staff will provide technical support for M&E activities including the HMIS and malaria reference centers. Two visits are planned to ensure adequate follow up of planned activities.
SUBTOTAL M&E		2,175,000	0		

OPERATIONAL RESEARCH

					Description
No planned activities			0	0	No operational research studies are planned with FY 2016 funding
SUBTOTAL OR			0	0	
IN-COUNTRY STAFFING AND ADMINISTRATION					
CDC	CDC IAA	550,000	0		Management, CDC resident advisor's salary.
USAID	USAID	1,659,916	0		Management and administration costs, USAID resident advisor and three FSN salaries, CDC and USAID RAs' ICASS costs, and 2% program development and learning
SUBTOTAL IN-COUNTRY STAFFING		2,209,916	0		
GRAND TOTAL		33,000,000	15,730,126